"I Teached Him to Talk"

Stories of Young Children with Autism

"I Teached Him to Talk":
Stories of
Young Children
with Autism

Marion VanArsdell

Copyright © 2017 Marion VanArsdell

All rights reserved including the right of reproduction in whole or in part in any form.

Cover design by Glenn Ruga/Visual Communications

Levellers Press, Amherst, Massachusetts

Printed in the United States of America

ISBN 978-1-945473-49-4

This book is dedicated to the children and families who taught me so much over the years and enriched my life enormously.

In loving memory of

My parents Gene and Jean Kenyon Bartlett

and

Barbara Carle, gifted teacher, storyteller and friend

Contents

Preface	ix
Introduction: The Retirement Tea	xiii
The First Year	1
The Second Year	51
Appendix: Information about the Classroom Model	143
Author's Appreciation	150

Preface

This book was written for parents who have been told that the child you love with all your heart falls somewhere along what is now called the autism spectrum. You may have been the first to suspect that something was not quite right in your child's development. Sometimes when you voiced your concerns to your pediatrician you were advised to wait and watch how your child did over the next several months. Sooner or later, your child was referred for an evaluation and has now been given a diagnosis of autism spectrum disorder (ASD).

Now you are searching the internet and bookstores for information and ideas about how to help your child. Most of all you are looking for hope.

This book is also for the grandparents, family members and friends who love your child and want to support you in the weeks and years ahead. It is for teachers and therapists too, because you may well find that the children in these stories remind you of ones who intrigue and challenge you every day.

"I Teached Him to Talk" is a collection of stories chronicling two years in an intensive public school program for three to five year old children with ASD. These stories are based on real children and true events but to respect the privacy of children and families, their names, identifying features and specific time frames have been changed.

Luis came to school at three years of age with a vocabulary of only three words. Teddy arrived soon after speaking in full sentences that we often couldn't understand because of his unique articulation patterns. Luis fascinated and scared Teddy in equal measure. They were just settling into an uneasy alliance when James joined the class and began a "race to be first" that would last for months.

Luis, Teddy and James are the main characters in the first year of this book. These are their stories and those of the children who came next. Adam spoke in odd quotations and repeated things that were said to him but could not create an original sentence or answer simple questions. We soon discovered he could read, leading his mother to wonder out loud, "How can a four year old read when he can't even talk?"

Although they shared a common diagnosis, each child had a unique combination of strengths and challenges. Our job was to understand them better so that we could design learning opportunities that capitalized on their strengths to help them make significant progress. The program combined a half day in a small class for intensive teaching with an afternoon preschool to integrate the children into a larger social group.

In order to address the individual needs of each child, we incorporated strategies from three different teaching approaches. The TEACCH Program from the University of North Carolina informed our model for structured teaching using visual schedules and a systematic, individualized work system. In accordance with the practices of Applied Behavior Analysis, discrete trials were included to help children master sequential language, cognitive and motor skills. The "Floortime" model developed by Dr. Stanley Greenspan and Dr. Serena Weider was used to build social skills and reciprocal language.

As you will see from these stories, the development of the program model was an interactive process. The team of teachers and therapists were always evaluating the effectiveness of the program and making modifications as needed. So this book is also the story of our teaching strategies, our best laid plans, and of what we tried next when some of those plans did not go at all as we had hoped.

These are stories of children who were often puzzling because so much of the world was a puzzle to them. They are children who struggled every day to make sense of a world that often seemed too full of sensation and language that they couldn't understand. They are children who were sometimes challenging to teach because they were constantly challenged by the world around them.

Introduction: The Retirement Tea

"Have you forgotten me?" Katherine asks when I walk over to greet her today at the tea held in the school library at the end of a busy day.

"Of course I haven't forgotten you," I say in response to Katherine's question. "I would never forget you."

I'd been surprised to see Katherine and Jonathan standing with their mothers at the back of the crowded library. Children, parents and colleagues are gathered to honor three of us who are retiring in a few days. Katherine and Jonathan are students from the earlier years in my career teaching young children with special needs so I'm amazed to see them here today. As soon as the short speeches are over, I make my way to greet them.

Jonathan doesn't ask if I've forgotten him; that would not be his style. I reach out to shake his hand and he greets me with a shy smile.

"Jonathan, it's a nice surprise to see you here. Thank you for coming."

"You're welcome," he says and I see that he's holding two photos in his hands. When I ask to see the pictures, he hands me one that shows him standing next to a large rock in front of a building on his college campus.

"He graduated two weeks ago," his mother announces proudly and I answer that I thought he still had one more year to go.

"No I'm all done and I passed every course," he says with pride.

He gives me the other picture and I'm surprised to see their preschool class photo of years ago with Katherine in the front row and

Jonathan looking straight into the camera from the middle row. I think back to the little boy who put every puzzle piece in his mouth and wouldn't say a word on his first visit to school all those years ago.

Jonathan was a beautiful three year old with light brown bangs framing darker brown eyes that seemed to be looking off in the distance. On the day he visited our busy preschool classroom for an evaluation, we hadn't heard him say a single word by the time the children finished playing and sat down for a snack. As luck would have it, we sat him at one of the low round tables next to Laura, a very talkative three year old.

Laura took it upon herself to strike up a conversation with the visiting boy and began by asking him his name. Jonathan didn't answer so Laura asked if he wanted a cookie. Although he didn't say a word, Jonathan reached over and took a cookie off the plate. Laura talked on and even began using some of the signs she had learned because another child in the class used sign language instead of speech. Nothing seemed to be working as Jonathan didn't say a word. Finally, in frustration, Laura began to look around the room and randomly name items in the environment.

"Say table," she said to Jonathan, tapping one hand on the table where they sat. When he didn't respond, she went on to ask him to name the floor, a cup, a chair and the window. Jonathan sat silent beside her but Laura persisted.

"Say radiator," she said pointing across the room.

As it turned out, that was a topic of particular interest to Jonathan, so he looked in the direction she was pointing and called out excitedly, "Radiator."

"I did it," Laura exclaimed, raising her arms in the air. "I teached him to talk!"

Soon after Jonathan began in our class, he was joined by Katherine. Every day Katherine walked up the hill to school with her mother, flapping a yellow rubber glove in front of her sturdy little body. Unlike Jonathan, Katherine talked often but most of what she said was echolalic speech. She echoed words she heard, repeating lines from commercials on T.V. and favorite videos that she had memorized, but never used original phrases or sentences.

One morning soon after Katherine started school, the principal came into our classroom to talk with me for a minute. The principal, a tall and statuesque woman, was always very stylishly dressed. Since I was sitting on the floor with children, she leaned over to talk with me. As she did, her rope of white beads swung gently out in front of her.

Suddenly Katherine came running across the room, lifted the beads up a little in both of her hands and said, "Just the right touch."

"Why, thank you," the principal said smiling in response to this unexpected compliment.

We never told the principal that Katherine was repeating a line from Cinderella spoken by the birds when the beads are draped on Cinderella's gown for the ball. For Katherine, the string of beads had called up an association and she spoke the line that matched that picture in her memory bank. To the principal it seemed like a spontaneous compliment but we knew that it was an example of the scripts that Katherine carried around in her head.

Eighteen years later Jonathan is a college graduate. His mother tells me that the picture of Jonathan at college was taken after he spoke at a symposium on disability awareness. He talked about what it is like to have Asperger Syndrome and what he's learned about how his mind works.

Now Katherine is a young woman who works two jobs each day, sometimes supervised by a job coach as she gains work experience.

"Which job do you like better, Katherine?" I ask.

"Oh I like them both," she answers. Katherine likes to work and uses her strong memory for detail as she learns to do filing and clerical work.

She remembers the birth dates of my three grandchildren and runs through them now even though we haven't seen each other for months. I remember her yellow rubber glove and all of her echolalic language. Now she is having a conversation with me, telling me that her younger sister has graduated from high school. Later when we have a minute alone, her mother tells me that they are noticing new capabilities in Katherine all the time.

"We used to think she would reach her limit and stop learning," she says. "Instead it seems that she just keeps on making progress."

Jonathan and Katherine didn't have the diagnosis of autism in the late 1980's; that would come much later when they were in fifth grade. They were both found to have special needs but it was just called "developmental delays" in those days. Both children came into our integrated preschool right along with everybody else; the typical children chosen by lottery, peers with language delay, cerebral palsy, hearing loss, visual impairment and other special needs.

Autism was reserved for children like Lisa, a child at an earlier school, who stood at the top of the stairs in the corner of the classroom and danced back and forth from foot to foot. Lisa hummed when she was happy and made odd little sounds of distress when she was not. She fit our picture of autism and, when we heard that diagnosis, we didn't expect as much of her or of ourselves as we should have.

We know so much more now than we did when Katherine and Jonathan came through our classroom door. Now there is a wide range of strategies for teaching children on the autism spectrum. Competing philosophies and approaches offer rich options and we are not limited to any one way. We pull from them what seems to work best for each child though we certainly have a central model that we follow and adapt as needed. In the days of Katherine and Jonathan we were often "flying by the seat of our pants", trusting that what we were doing for all the children in the class would, over time, work for them too. Indeed all that their families and teachers have done to teach and support them over the years has worked for them and here they are today, two young adults marking my retirement.

The puzzle of autism didn't claim my attention all at once, it happened over time. Thinking back on my years of teaching, I realize that autism came into my life gradually, one child at a time. Jonathan and Katherine were the first of the children with autism, even though we didn't call them autistic at the time. They were followed by one child after another who challenged the way I was teaching and the way we had designed the preschool programs for our school system. The "one size fits all" model we had did not do enough for children on the autism spectrum who don't learn incidentally; who don't spontaneously imitate their peers and often don't even seem to pay attention to them.

Parents who had become fierce advocates for their children were an important part of what could be called my awakening. They weren't willing to settle for a program that was offering only ten hours a week at school. They wanted and sometimes demanded more hours and more specialized interventions for their child. They had been reading about children who made progress with more intensive programs and about the critical importance of early intervention.

They were passionate about wanting more for their children and soon I became a partner in that passion, questioning what we were doing and eager to find out more. This fascination with how children on the autism spectrum learn or don't learn was what drove me to take a year off to spend my time visiting leading research centers, attending workshops and courses, and immersing myself in the study of educational models for young children with autism. It was a time to visit different kinds of programs, to flit around the edge of sometimes warring camps and try to decide for myself what looked truest.

I came back to Northampton and designed a new program, supported by Dr. Isabelina Rodriquez, Director and Dr. Craig Jurgenson, Associate Director of Special Education. The program provided a full day at school for children from three to five years old who met the criteria for intensive intervention. The program was rich in teaching staff. I was the lead teacher and, in the years described in this book, we had two assistant teachers, Lilly Pastor and Maria de la Vega. Other teaching assistants worked with us in the years when we had more children and each person brought skills and insights that enriched the program. Eliza D'Agostino is an experienced Speech/Language Pathologist and she was instrumental in helping us develop this program. We were a new team when this program began so we were all learning together in those first years.

Early readers of this manuscript had varied opinions on how much background about autism and the design of this program is needed before readers approach the stories.

Some people felt more background is necessary but others were impatient with that and wanted to get right to the stories.

Recently I heard an interview with Mo Willems, the children's book author and illustrator. He said that in his writing, he always tries to think *about* his audience but he doesn't ever want to think *for* them.

I like that - so I will leave it to each reader to choose which way to go from here. If you are a teacher or parent and want more information on how we designed this program and why, then take some time and read the appendix that is at the end of the book. Otherwise just continue reading and meet the children.

This is the chronicle of our shared journey as the children often surprised us with their humor, their insights, their delight in things we would have missed and their ability to persist against tremendous odds.

The First Year

Luis

On the day I go to meet Luis for the first time, he is running around their apartment dressed in nothing but a diaper that glows white against the light brown tone of his sturdy three year old body. It's a cool September day so I'm surprised at first by his lack of clothes.

His mother Emily senses my curiosity and explains that because Luis doesn't like the feel of clothing on his body or of socks or shoes on his feet, he usually sheds whatever clothes are put on him. He's learned to tolerate clothes and shoes to go outside but immediately strips down to his diaper as soon as he comes home, leaving a trail of clothes as he moves across the living room.

When I arrive Luis is climbing over the back of the couch and dropping down head first into the deep brown corduroy. His muscular tan legs balance for just a moment before they come down onto the rug as he does a lopsided somersault. He's in almost constant motion as I talk with his mother and learn more about the concerns she first voiced to their pediatrician months after Luis turned two.

Luis runs into the other room, comes back carrying an armful of brightly colored bears and begins to carefully set one bear at a time up on the back of the couch. Then he runs around and dives head first over into the deep cushions, taking the bear along with him. He repeats this game until all of the bears have survived the dive and are lined up along the deep green area rug.

Trying to lure him to a quieter activity, Emily sets a bucket of small colored cubes on the top of a white desk that sits in one corner of their living room.

"Let's build," she says to Luis and, as soon as he sees the blocks, he settles into the little chair attached to the desk. It's the first time he's settled in one place since I arrived and his dark brown eyes follow his mother's hands as she reaches into the bucket.

"These are one of his favorite toys," she tells me. "It's one of the few things that he'll sit down and do for a little while." As she's talking, Emily begins stacking small cube blocks into a vertical tower, using various colors as she makes the tower taller. Luis watches her for a moment and Emily holds a blue square out to him.

"Put it on here, Luis," she says as she points to the top of her tower.

Instead Luis takes the blue block and sets it in front of him on the surface of the desk. Then he reaches into the box, finds another blue block and sets it on top of the first.

"Watch what he will do now," Emily says proudly, handing him a red cube. "He can match all the colors."

Sure enough, as soon as he has lined a red cube up next to the blue one, Luis reaches in and finds a matching red cube to set on top. His mother works next to him, handing him a new color each time and watching as Luis finds a matching block. Then he goes back and begins to add a third block, beginning with the blue set and working his way systematically through the colored array.

"Good work buddy," she says to him, reaching over to run her hand over his close cropped black hair. "He'll keep doing that until they're all in towers of one color," Emily says to me, "but you could see that he didn't like it when I mixed the colors in my tower."

As she speaks, Luis starts to disassemble her tower, moving each block over to one of the matching towers that spread out in front of him on the desk. I've been visiting for forty minutes and still haven't heard Luis say a word.

"He's really good at matching and sorting the blocks by color," I comment. "How about naming the colors, have you heard him do that yet?'

"Not really," she says. "That's the thing that worries me the most and Dr. Wright saw it too. Luis doesn't really talk so that's why we've had the therapist from the Early Intervention team coming to work with him here."

Luis' failure to develop language was one of the red flags that caused his pediatrician to refer him for a neurological evaluation. The combination of his language deficits, his repetitive patterns of play and his sensory issues led to Luis' diagnosis as a child with autism spectrum disorder or ASD.

By the end of this first home visit, there is no doubt in my mind that Luis is a candidate for our intensive preschool program. But I realize that Luis may have difficulty adjusting to the routines of school. Emily says he is not a morning person and going to school will mean being wakened on a schedule, driven to a completely new place and left with unfamiliar adults. It will also mean that he is expected to keep his clothes and shoes on all day!

Luis' mother does all she can to ease the transition by bringing him to visit the classroom several times and by driving him to school for the first few days. She also lets him bring a favorite toy or stuffed animal to school every day – a pattern that continues for months as various objects from home help him leave her behind and get on the van to school.

Once Luis starts school we discover that he is not completely without language. He has a vocabulary of three words delivered with varying intensity – "No" and "Shut Up."

"No," he yells when Lilly first shows him his name card and tries to coax him to come and sit in one of the brightly colored cube chairs for music circle.

But soon he can't resist his own drive to match the name card on his cubby with the identical name on his schedule board, posted about six feet away. It's a place to start and for days that is all he will do. He won't take the next card with the picture for music circle and go to the rug. Instead he sits in his cubby, holding whatever toy or stuffed animal he brought from home and watches music circle from a safe distance. We go on with the other children who take turns choosing a song by selecting a picture card from the ones lined up on the easel.

Every so often, Lilly goes over and sits for a minute next to Luis. "Music time," she says quietly, holding up a card with the icon for music.

"Shut up," Luis shouts, glaring at her through squinted dark eyes as he crosses both arms across his chest and turns away from her. But soon we begin to notice times when he claps his hands or stamps his feet almost in time with the other children.

Then one morning after Luis has been at school for several weeks, he walks calmly over to the music circle, puts his music picture card up on the board next to the other children's cards and sits down in the yellow cube chair, holding his blue Care Bear tightly in his lap. For the next year he spends in the class, Luis will establish his exclusive right to always sit in the yellow chair.

Once he comes to morning circle, we start to work with Luis on the first common social question. We begin circle every day by asking each child their name and the other two boys quickly answer with some approximation of their name.

"What is your name?" I ask Luis.

"Name," he repeats.

"What is *your name*?" I ask again, pointing to him for emphasis.

Maria cues him from where she is sitting behind his chair. "Say Luis," Maria says quietly.

This immediately annoys Luis and he turns to look directly at her. "No" he says with an angry voice, "Shut up," using his entire vocabulary before turning his back on all of us.

For days we repeat the question every morning, asking each child in turn. When we come to Luis, I ask the question just once and wait before modeling the answer for him. Finally one morning when I ask the question, Luis pauses for just a moment before tapping his right hand on his chest and saying, "Luis."

Maria, Lilly and I all smile at each other in recognition of this milestone, and Luis smiles back at us, still holding the palm of one hand to his chest.

* * *

Luis comes to the low blue table for individual work with a teacher before he ever joins music circle. The bait is set out on the shelf next to the table in brightly colored workboxes using the TEACCH model for structured teaching. I choose colored cube blocks like the ones I'd seen him sort at home for the first box, then markers and white paper, and a puzzle with trucks and cars – each task in its own box.

Attracted by materials he likes, Luis takes the bait and we begin to teach him the routine to take one box at a time from the shelf on his left and set the work out on the table in front of him.

Luis loves to work with these favorite things but we soon learn that he often wants to repeat the same task over and over rather than moving it into the "all done basket" on the floor to the right of his chair. When he takes the box with paper and markers down and begins to work, there is no stopping Luis. He won't stop until every paper is completely covered with color.

"Difficulty shifting attention" is the term used to describe the way that children with autism spectrum disorders lock on to an activity or topic and cannot easily change tracks. Once we recognize this in Luis' behavior, we realize that we need to develop strategies to help him anticipate the end of one thing and transition to the next. We learn to put only two pieces of paper in the drawing box to limit the amount of time he needs to spend on that task. Our priority at first is to build a trusting relationship with Luis and to make school a good experience so he will want to come and engage with the adults and children in the class.

Because Luis is such a visual learner, we begin the labor-intensive process of teaching him how to exchange a picture card for something he wants to eat at snack time. At the beginning, a single picture card of a favorite food is on the table in front of him and we teach him to hand that card to a teacher to request the snack he wants. The Picture Exchange Communication System (PECS) has proven to be an effective way to help some children with autism use their visual interest and skills to build communication. It is a slow and labor intensive process to teach a child to use pictures to communicate but for many children it becomes a bridge to verbal communication.

Once Luis is using his cards to make requests, we teach him to expand his communication to include comments, beginning first with the things that fascinate him. The sound of a lawnmower anywhere around the school grounds always draws him to the windows along one side of the classroom. He runs back and forth, his hands moving rhythmically up and down with excitement. Almost every day the engines from the nearby fire station come up the street, lights flashing and siren blaring. Luis usually hears the siren before any of us can and begins his excited pacing back and forth, looking sideways out the window.

We make a board with a picture strip at the top and the words "I see" above the drawing of a face with big eyes wide open and an arrow pointing away from the black eyes. Underneath this there is a velcro strip holding picture cards of a lawnmower, fire truck, car, van, and pickup truck. When Luis is attracted to the window by the sounds of a vehicle, one of the teaching staff joins him there and follows with the "I see" board.

"Look, fire truck" we say, pointing out the window at the fire truck and then at the card with the red fire engine. We put the card up in line with the words and speak the sentence to him, "I see fire truck." Gradually Luis begins to pick the right card himself, put it in place and eventually tries to imitate our sentence.

* * *

At first he learns everything like that, with the slow and deliberate teaching of one small step at a time to build his understanding of language. We teach him the names of objects by repetitively labeling the toys he chooses. We see his puzzled expression when we give him a simple direction so we learn to guide him through each action time and again until he begins to understand that words match certain actions.

"Touch head," we say touching our hands to our own heads, showing him over and over again until he can follow simple directions. Sometimes this means weathering his outbursts of frustration while trying to hold on to our own patience.

"No beads," Luis yells when he sees a task he doesn't like in one of his workboxes. When those words fail to get a response from the teacher working with him, he tries another approach. "All done beads" he says and takes the box from the shelf and puts it directly into the "all done" basket. Gradually he begins to use more words to communicate, although at times he uses his emerging language to refuse to do what we had planned for him.

Sometimes our patience wears thin and we can't come up with a strategy for enlisting Luis' cooperation. But Lilly is often a master at finding a way around his initial resistance. One day Lilly sits across the low blue table from him presenting picture cards for action words, an exercise designed to help him learn verbs so that he can combine a noun and verb to make a simple sentence. He is absorbed in coloring circles on a big piece of paper when Lilly holds up the first card, a photo of a boy climbing the ladder to a slide.

"Luis, what is he doing?"

Luis looks at the picture for just a moment, returns to his coloring and announces, "No up."

"Climbing up" Lilly says and he takes a quick look at the picture again.

"No climbing up" he says.

Lilly holds up the next card with a picture of a boy licking a popsicle. "What's he doing?" she asks again. Luis sticks out his tongue and makes slurping noises.

"Yes" Lilly says with animation. "He's eating a popsicle."

"No eating popsicle," Luis protests, choosing an orange marker for the next circle. On it goes, one card after another with Lilly's statement followed by Luis shouting "No" and then repeating the verb.

"No riding bike." "No washing hands." "No drinking."

Lilly has found a way through his resistance by just going ahead and showing him one card after another. Each attempt at an answer is preceded by Luis' loud and emphatic "No," but he then goes on to repeat each verb after Lilly. Verbs with negation – but verbs all the same!

Teddy Arrives on the Scene

I am first introduced to Teddy on paper when his evaluation reports arrive on my desk. The real Teddy captures my heart within minutes of my arrival at his house for an initial home visit. Dressed in a bright blue tie-dyed shirt that captures the color of his eyes, he is circling around from hall to living room riding a small wooden giraffe. Teddy is tall for his age so the toy giraffe doesn't really fit him anymore and his knees stick up high above the seat. Around and around he goes with increased excitement until his father calls him over to where a bucket of toy cars sit on a shelf.

"Come over here, Teddy," he calls, "Let's play with your cars."

Teddy isn't immediately ready to stop his wild ride until his father gives him the idea that he can park the giraffe right next to the cars. With that cue, he wheels over and lines the giraffe up carefully next to the little rug that has roads and garages laid out in the design of a city. Teddy flops down on the floor next to his father, his sturdy legs spread wide in the W pattern that is a red flag for low muscle tone. I haven't heard Teddy say a word until he sits down and his father asks him which car he wants first.

"I want the dew tar," Teddy says and his father rummages through the cars until he comes up with a blue car and hands it to Teddy. Teddy holds the car in one hand while he crawls awkwardly around the rug looking for the right place to park this first car. He finally settles on the outline of a parking space in front of the post office.

"They must be going to mail a letter," his father comments.

"Yes, a yetter to Gwammy," Teddy says with a big smile.

This is my introduction to Teddy's language. He has many more words and understands language far better than Luis but his immature articulation often makes it difficult to understand him. We soon learn that this is a sensitive issue for Teddy.

When Teddy begins in our class, we don't need to use a picture communication system because he already has a good start on developing language. But his ability to communicate effectively is often limited by his unusual way of articulating words. Sometimes we are completely puzzled by a phrase he uses and have to ask his parents for help translating. It's frustrating for Teddy when we can't understand what he is saying because he is smart enough to see through the general answers we revert to when we can't figure out what he's saying.

Snack time usually goes smoothly because the choices are right there in front of us so we can understand what Teddy wants. One day during his second week of school, when he asks for "goose" at snack time, Maria decides it is a good chance to help him work on his articulation. She points to her own rounded lips and says, "Say juice." Teddy's face immediately changes and he bursts into sobs.

Maria is completely surprised by this intense response to her gentle suggestion. "It's alright, Teddy," she says over and over as she rubs his back until he calms down and has a drink of "goose".

After a little while Maria says, "You were sad when I asked you to say juice." Teddy's lips begin to quiver when he hears the word sad. "It's alright sometimes to feel sad," Maria consoles him, "but now you are okay."

This is our introduction to Teddy's discomfort or fear of feeling sad. When we write a note home about the "goose" event, his parents write back that Teddy has been having a very strong reaction to things that make him sad. He loves to have books read to him but they have had to put some books away because Teddy finds them too sad right now. They often have music playing while they drive in the car, but Teddy now begins to cry when certain songs come on.

From then on as disappointments come up in the class or other children get upset about something, we begin to use these daily events as a way to talk with Teddy about being sad. Our general theme was stated simply in Maria's first response to him. "It's alright to feel sad – later you will be okay."

Teddy hears our words but it is clear that he is not at all sure this is true. When a disappointment or intense feeling catches him by surprise, he's not convinced that he *will* be okay anytime soon.

Luis, Teddy and the Care Bears

One morning soon after Teddy joins our group, Luis arrives at school with yet another Care Bear. He walks quickly through the foyer and past the glass windows that line the front wall of the office. As always he is getting ahead of me as we make our way from his van to our classroom.

As soon as we are in our room, Luis goes right over to his yellow cube chair for music time, the new green bear in tow.

"Who's first?" I ask, getting ready to begin the morning greeting song.

"Care Bear's turn," Luis announces holding the bear on his lap.

No sooner have we starting singing "Hello Bear, Hello Bear" when Luis interrupts us saying, "NO…. Laugh a Lot Bear."

So we all begin the song again singing the correct name. Teddy thinks that this name is very funny, and Luis surprises us by pressing Care Bear's paw until it begins to emit a strange electronic laughing sound.

"You touched Care Bear's hand," I say, trying to interject some vocabulary drill. Luis begins to touch body parts on his bear and we label them together. "Hands, eyes, nose, hair, legs, feet."

"What's this?" I ask, turning the bear over and pointing to the short orange tail.

"Funny bone," Luis announces loudly and that sends Teddy into a delighted laugh.

"Funny bone," he repeats over and over again, adding it to the surprising phrases he is learning from Luis.

During afternoon circle we introduce a new song - a silly song with rhyming words. We look at the song poster I illustrated some years ago as we sing through verses about a fox in a box, a frog and a dog in a log. Then we begin the last verse – the silliest of all.

"I heard a cow say meow," I sing and the children join in. Teddy loves it, always one to enjoy the humor in any situation.

But Luis begins to protest loudly. "No meow," he says emphatically. "Cow … Moo!"

We move on to the next line in the hope that we can get through this song.

We sing "Then he says 'bow-wow,'" and most of the children laugh at this absurdity.

But Luis will have none of it. "No bow-wow," he says, shaking his head. "Cow…moo." He has been working entirely too hard learning labels and animal sounds to tolerate this confusion.

So I hurry us along to the last verse as I point to the picture of the whale and the snail.

"Dolphin," Luis says eagerly, standing up so he can come and point to the whale as he emits a low, haunting sound.

"Hey, I heared that on my video," Teddy says excitedly, impressed by Luis' ability to imitate the sound of a dolphin.

"Yes, dolphin," Luis says proudly as he sits back down in his yellow cube chair.

"Yes Tiger"

Luis is not a morning person and usually does not speak for at least fifteen minutes after the time we greet his van and welcome him to school. We say a cheerful "Good morning" addressing him by name and often add that we are glad to see him, but Luis says nothing. He greets us with a scowl if he's had a hard morning and with just the hint of a grin on his best days.

But this morning, when the door of the red van slides open, there he sits rubbing tears from his eyes as he announces, "Sad."

It is a remarkable thing for this child of daily ups and downs to label a feeling – his feeling – spontaneously and in context.

Then Luis points toward the front seat of the van and says, "Want tigers please."

The story soon unfolds as the van driver tells us of the misbehavior that led to her taking the two stuffed tigers he brought with him from home and putting them out of his view in the front seat of the van. We negotiate for the tigers to be restored to him and Luis is easily persuaded to go to the playground before we go into our room for music circle.

"Always" is not really a concept that makes sense in this classroom. No one is that consistent. Sometimes it works to let Luis bring the stuffed animal of the day to music circle; sometimes he will still pay attention. Today because he already lost the tigers once on the van, I decide to let him bring one tiger over to music circle and I am flexible enough to incorporate his tiger into the morning greeting song. Luis holds the tiger up with two front paws extended to me so I can hold Tiger's paws just as I hold each child's hands while we sing good morning to them. When we are done singing "Hello Tiger," I say quietly, "Luis' turn."

Luis accepts this, tucking the tiger behind him in the chair, and gives me his hands so that I can sing to him. Later when it's time to make the transition to his work time, Lilly decides to hide his tiger because she knows from experience that it will probably distract him from doing the tasks on his plan for the day. She manages to take the tiger and hide it behind her coat while Luis is busy pushing the yellow chair over to his table.

But of course he asks for his tiger as soon as he settles into his work area. When Lilly tells him that tiger is all gone, Luis goes on strike, pushing back into the corner of his work area on the rug, refusing to sit in his favorite yellow chair and alternately crying and yelling.

Trying to explain that it is time to work first and then he can have his tiger back, Lilly pulls out a blue poster board strip that has the words *First* and *Then* printed with black marker. She attaches the card for work time under the word "*First*" and then pulls out a card with a tiger on it and puts that under the word "*Then*". She holds it down to where Luis is still sitting squeezed into the corner with his back against the shelf next to his table.

"First work, then tiger," she says.

"No work" he yells, trying to rip that icon from the board.

Lilly pulls it away just in time and points to each picture again in turn, "First work, then tiger."

This is when we realize that in spite of work we have been doing to teach the concept of *first/then*, Luis still doesn't understand. He thinks that Lilly is holding up a choice board like the ones we use sometimes to help him choose an activity.

"Yes tiger," he says as he touches the card with the picture of the tiger on it and moves to sit in his yellow chair at the table.

"I want tiger," he says producing a spontaneous three-word sentence when Lilly does not respond to his touching the card.

Luis is doing what we taught him will get results. He has stopped crying and yelling. He is talking but we are not honoring his communication. This goes against everything he's come to expect from us over the weeks since he started school. This boy who was lost in a sea of language has been learning that things have labels and people have names. And if he can remember a label and use it, he usually gets the thing he requested because we want him to see that communication is powerful

But because we have decided that the tiger is a distraction, we are not behaving as expected. No wonder his frustration is mounting. This is one of many times when a teacher has to make a decision about what the most important goal is for a child. Lilly realizes that this is a time to honor Luis' request and reward the way he has calmed himself down and is using words to ask for what he wants. She retrieves the tiger from its hiding place and hands it across the table to Luis.

"Yes tiger," Luis says as he sets the soft animal next to him in the yellow chair and reaches across to take the first workbox down from the shelf beside him.

"Whose Side Are You On?"

Luis' language is expanding and he now uses a variety of phrases he has memorized. Unfortunately his words and his meaning are often at odds with each other.

"Happy new year!" Luis called out in the middle of circle time today. "You clean up that mess!" he yelled earlier when Teddy carried Luis' backpack to the playground and set it on the sidewalk in front of him.

"Oh sorry, Marion," he says now as he walks beside me on his way to find the stencils and markers. "Close the door," he commands as he stands in front of the cupboard he wants me to unlock so he can look for his favorite rainbow stencil

But sometimes now there *is* a match between the words he says and his intent. "Go home NOW," he cried on Thursday when he missed the bus and his mother broke the routine by driving him to school. It was a match; he'd found the right words to say exactly what he wanted to do.

Luis is also beginning to use language more spontaneously. This morning at the playground, he calls out from the platform at the top of the climber.

"Lilly – come here."

When she goes up the stairs to stand beside him, Luis points to the opening in the tunnel slide and says, "Try this."

Lilly follows his lead and they take turns going down the slide and then climbing back up the stairs with Luis calling out and directing Lilly. She follows his directions, rewarding his language with her actions.

But then the next time she comes down the slide, Lilly sits up too soon at the bottom and bumps her head hard on the top of the tunnel.

"Ouch" she says and pretends to cry. This captures Luis' full attention.

"Hey" he says, "you crying?"

"Yes" she says rubbing her eyes with her fists, "I'm crying because I bumped my head."

"Hey," he says, "You crying – shut up."

He doesn't say this with an angry voice. It is just another of the phrases that he has in his repertoire, some odder than others.

"Hey, thank you very much!" he keeps shouting in an angry voice later on the playground, pointing his finger at the substitute teacher who just told him not to push another child.

At rest time, Luis suddenly calls across to Maria as she is rubbing another child's back.

"Whose side are you on?" he asks her in one of his seemingly random phrases.

Like so many children with autism, Luis has memorized phrases or lines he has learned from a cartoon or video, and uses them at times that don't necessarily make sense at first to the listener. He learns language in chunks but can't break those sentences apart to use the words more functionally. So we are often left trying to figure out what he is trying to communicate.

For days, whenever he was mad at one of us, he would point one finger at the offending teacher and say, "Good day, sir. I mean good day."

We were all at a loss as to why he used this phrase, although his affect made it quite clear what he meant to communicate. Then one day Lilly came in and said that her grandson Raymond had been watching the video of Charlie and the Chocolate Factory and she heard Willy use that line whenever he wanted to get rid of Charlie. Luis had pulled this line from his memory bank and was correctly associating it with his feeling of wanting to be rid of a teacher's interference.

* * *

Today we learn that Luis is making the transition to using language more functionally. We have a substitute teacher with us because Maria is out sick, and I ask the new person to work with Luis this morning during individual work time. When music circle is over and he pushes his yellow chair over to his table, she goes over and sits down across from Luis.

"Stand up," he says to her.

She doesn't respond and takes the first workbox down and sets it on the low table between them.

He tries again. "Stand up," he says. But the substitute sits tight and takes the puzzle out, spreading the loose pieces on the table in front of him.

Now Luis calls across the room to where Lilly is working with another child.

"Hey Lilly," he calls trying to get her attention. She ignores him at first but after several repetitions, all delivered in an unusually calm tone of voice, she stands up and looks over the shelf that blocks her view of Luis.

"Come here," he says as soon as he catches her eye.

Lilly walks over and stands beside his table to see what he needs; leaving the child she is with to work independently for a few minutes.

Again Luis turns his attention to the unfamiliar adult across the table from him. His voice is louder this time as he repeats, "Stand up."

This time the substitute teacher follows his direction and, as soon as she stands up, a smile spreads across Luis' face.

Turning to Lilly, he points to the empty chair across from him and says, "Sit down."

With six words he has executed a plan and moved the staff around to suit his pleasure. We have been working to teach Luis to follow commands, using repeated trials to teach him the meaning of common directions. Now he has taken three of those directions and used them very functionally to achieve his goal. Lilly stays and the substitute walks over to work with the other child. With a wide smile and a twinkle in his dark eyes, Luis settles into work with Lilly, pleased with the power of this new tool - language.

Luis and the Afternoon Kids

"Blue," Luis cries out first, pointing to the picture of blue water that covers the lower third of the page I am holding out for the class to see. I read on for a line or two. "Green," Luis announces for the next page. "Yes," I say, "the frogs are green." "Brown," he calls out next. "Brown toad," Sarah says from her spot next to him on the rug. "Brown toad," he repeats.

This truly unorthodox reading of a story goes on with ten children following the story line and Luis calling out colors for each page. It has the quality of a call and response song.

Later Luis is sitting at one of the trapezoid tables with two other children during a drawing activity. He loves "coloring" and eagerly comes with the others to small group time when he sees that they will be coloring. He has one set of markers in front of him and has gathered a small pile of white paper. He takes out a blue marker and carefully draws a vertical line from a third of the way down the paper all the way to the bottom. Then he takes a second color and draws an identical line next to the first. He repeats this until he has eight vertical lines on the piece of paper, one line of each color in the set of markers.

Allie, a calm girl with light brown hair and serious eyes, is sitting next to him drawing a picture of all the members of her family, naming each one as she finishes a figure. She keeps looking over to see what Luis is doing. When he has a line of each color, he picks out the blue marker again and carefully draws a circle on top of the first line. Looking over at Allie, he smiles for a moment, points to the circle and carefully, if somewhat oddly, enunciates the word "bah-loon." Then he finds the next color and begins to draw a circle to match the second line.

"Hey Lilly," he calls across the room, "come here – look bah-loons". Lilly bends down for a minute and quietly says something to him.

In September, Luis could not hold on to the word for balloon and always asked for them in speech therapy by pointing to the drawer where they were visible and asking for "yellow" or "purple". Now here he is announcing "bah-loon" each time he adds another circle to his picture.

A few minutes later I look over and see Allie ask him, "Luis, can I have a piece of paper?"

"Of course," he says, pulling a paper out of his pile and handing it to her.

She begins to draw lines of each color on her page. Luis looks up from his fierce concentration on his own work and notices what Allie is doing.

"Bah-loons?" he asks with a sudden smile.

"Yes, balloons for me too," she says, beginning to draw circles on the top of each of her colored lines.

Visitors from the Ukraine

This morning we have eight visitors from the Ukraine who are visiting our school as part of a two-week seminar on services for children with special needs. They had heard about our program for children with autism and asked if they could visit.

At first I go out in the hall to talk with them, showing them the picture schedules, the communication books and the visual cues for the work system that we use. They ask questions through an interpreter, eager for more information.

Through the window to the hall, the visitors can see Luis and Teddy sitting at two separate tables each doing their independent work. Luis has finished the puzzle that was in his first box. Now he is using an alphabet board with lower case letters painted onto wooden circles that he is supposed to fit into the round spaces with the matching upper case letters. Instead he is sorting the round circles by color and building towers with them.

I ask the visitors if they would like to go into the classroom, and as soon as the question is translated, many of them smile and respond eagerly. So I open the door and the troop of eight visitors wearing headphones for translation follow me into the room.

Luis looks up from his table and breaks into an immediate smile when he sees the crowd of visitors enter the room. Looking up at them, he puts his right hand on his chest and announces, "I…Luis."

Immediately one of the women closest to him bends down, holds out her hand to him and says her name. Luis takes the hand she extends in his right hand for a minute, not sure what to do with it. Then he raises his arm to point over the shelf to where Teddy is working.

"Say 'Hi Teddy,'" he instructs the eight Ukrainians. They don't understand this so he stands up for emphasis and points to me.

"Say 'Hi Marion,'" he says and this time the translator understands what he is asking. As soon as this is relayed through the headphones, the eight visitors comply with his request and greet me by name.

Satisfied with this result, Luis sits back down and begins dismantling the two towers, this time beginning to scan the board in front of him for the matching space for each letter.

A Force to Be Reckoned With

Teddy and Luis have just begun to build a fragile alliance when James, a force to be reckoned with, joins our group.

James has been in the regular preschool program since September after he was referred because of difficulty processing or understanding language and limited expressive language. His teacher Louise Homstead and Eliza D"Agostino, the Speech/Language Pathologist, were very concerned that James' language was developing in unusual patterns. They also observed James' rigidity as he was easily upset when his way of playing with toys is interrupted by another child.

I observe James in his class for the first time in November. When I come into the room, he's working alone at a small table with a large basket of colored bristle blocks he chose from the shelf. James is carefully building identical towers by using the same pattern of colors for each one. When another child tries to join him at the table and build following her own ideas, James is indignant and manages to scare the other child away. Sharing is not on James' agenda.

Transitions are difficult for James and he succeeds in making them difficult for everyone around him. He often falls on the floor and cries loudly when he is told it is time to finish a favorite activity and come to circle time. The longer he is in preschool, the clearer it becomes to Eliza and Louise that there is more going on for James than his language problems.

His parents are originally from Europe and both teach at colleges in the area. When I meet them for the first time, they share their concerns about James' behavior at home. He has a brother in college and a sister in high school and both usually try to cater to what James wants. But James' demands often exhaust their flexibility and good will, so it is impossible to prevent outbursts that make it difficult to take James on family outings.

James' parents asked their pediatrician for help in understanding his needs and she had referred him to a neurologist for an evaluation. The neurologist concluded that James is a child on the autism spectrum and recommended that he have more intensive services. At a Team Meeting with his parents it's decided that James continue in his regular afternoon preschool but that he also attend our intensive special needs preschool each morning.

* * *

On James' first day attending our class, music time goes very smoothly. He comes right over to the rug and joins in several of his favorite songs. I know from his parents and from Louise that James loves to sing. But I should know better than to assume that the second day will proceed smoothly from the first.

On the second day things take a wrong turn with Luis just before James walks through the door. For the last week, Luis has arrived every morning clutching a blue Thomas engine in one hand and a new green Percy in the other, sometimes also juggling the red car he calls "Christmas caboose". Things go awry when I casually say something to Luis about putting his Thomas train away in his backpack. I should know better! He is not about to put them away in his backpack and goes on strike in front of his cubby, refusing for the moment to come over to music time.

When James comes into the room, he probably would have headed right over to the music circle but he is immediately attentive to Luis' model of defiance. When he sees Luis resisting, James heads for the far end of the classroom and calls his own refusal across the room. One of our goals for the children in the class is that they learn to imitate the play of other children - but this is not what we had in mind! James is now imitating behavior we wish he would ignore. Luis' refusal is exciting to him and he decides to try that out instead of just coming on over and singing. We are caught in a dilemma because if we keep trying to persuade them to come, we are giving our attention to their refusals and may well end up reinforcing the very behavior we want to discourage.

So we go ahead and begin the circle without them, singing good morning to Teddy who has been patiently waiting for the drama to unfold and thankfully has not decided to add his own refusal to the mix. After we sing to Teddy we sing to each of the teaching staff. Then

I announce we will sing good morning to Thomas the Tank Engine next and that is all the hook Luis needs to run over to take in his place in the circle, Thomas in one hand and Percy in the other.

Of course, I know that I could be criticized for backing down because I have removed the demand that he put the trains away in his backpack. Instead I end up using the trains, singing to them to win Luis' cooperation. In one way he wins the battle but there is a long day ahead of us, and this seems to me a small price to pay for breaking the stalemate.

Now that Luis is over at music circle, he doesn't like it at all that James is not coming over to sit in the cube chair next to him.

"James," he calls across the room, "Come sit down,"

By now James is at the farthest corner of the classroom spinning the water wheel on the shelf near the water table. There is nothing more disturbing to an ex-offender than to see another child continue to break the rule.

"James, it's time for music," Luis calls across the room.

I decide to go ahead with the next song to hold Luis and Teddy's attention while Lilly goes and helps James move closer to the music circle. He comes to sit in a small rocking chair with his back to us all through Old MacDonald even though we know it is a favorite song. But when we bring out a felt board with an apple tree and bright green velour apples lined up below it, we have James' attention. We start the CD with a song about Farmer Brown and his apples and James is there, climbing over the back of his cube chair to join the circle.

Somehow the combination of the visual props and the CD captures James' attention. I don't know if it is the novelty or the familiarity of the song that brings him over.

"I'm first," he says, as he comes up to the felt board and attaches one of the green apples to the tree. I don't know it then but those two words, "I'm first", will come back to haunt us.

The Human Buffer Zone

By James' third week of school we decide to line the three cube chairs up on the rug for music time so that Teddy will be the human buffer zone between his two more volatile classmates, Luis and James. The yellow chair that Luis always wants to sit in is on one side of Teddy's chair and James' chair is on the other. We carefully leave a space between each chair because Teddy and Luis do not like anyone to sit too close to them. Luis particularly reacts immediately to anyone moving in on what he considers to be his space. Unfortunately James has an opposite need so, before he can settle in to the music circle, he tries to line his chair up right next to one of theirs with the sides touching.

On Monday morning James comes in to the room, hangs his coat in his cubby, takes his music card from his picture schedule and arrives at the rug just after Teddy has already settled himself in the middle chair. Instead of sitting in the red chair beside Teddy, James pushes and pulls the chair out of position and begins to move it around to the other side of Luis' vacant yellow chair. Lilly sees our plan unraveling and realizes that Luis and James seated next to each other will be an electric combination. She quickly positions herself on a small chair next to Luis, filling the space that James is moving toward with his red chair. Morning circle is quickly taking on the intrigue of a human chess game.

James is determined and tries different maneuvers to see if he can force his chair in between Lilly and Luis' chair. I explain to him that there is no space, and pointing to the vacant spot on the other side of Teddy, I say in what I hope is my most definitive teacher voice, "The red chair goes here."

Luis has been busy putting his things away and misses this whole exchange. He takes his card from the picture schedule and comes over to the rug announcing, "Time for music." He puts his music card on the one remaining Velcro dot on the easel and settles into his yellow chair.

James is still standing next to his red chair behind the other boys as I turn to point out the song choices for the day. When I turn back,

I see that James has planted his chair right behind the other two boys and is leaning forward with his head resting between Luis and Teddy's chairs. James is not smiling.

This proximity immediately begins to annoy Luis who does best with a clear zone around him on all sides so nothing and no one touches or surprises him. "Ouch, he pushed me," he yells when James leans in closer and his cheek grazes Luis' arm. The morning is off to a rough start for sure!

James spends most of the music time moving the red cube chair around, trying to get in line on the other side of Luis. Lilly holds her place and foils his plan but there is nothing relaxing about this time of singing. Soon James' frustration has been transmitted to us all.

It reminds me of the pictures they made at circle yesterday of three faces, one drawn by each child and then labeled with their description. The first two faces were "happy" by James and "sad" by Teddy. The third picture was by Luis who labeled it "mad", but then James called it "angry" and Teddy added "frustrated".

The day continues to go downhill from here and by the end of the day I declare it the worst day of our school year and leave for home feeling sad, mad, and frustrated, having lost my grip on "happy" somewhere along the way.

Teddy seems to roll along but every day this week has included times of stepping on the landmines of Luis' and James' firm resistance. No matter how much I can tell myself that this is rooted in their disability, their difficulty processing language and their need to feel in control, I am exhausted by the end of the day. I understand intellectually that this is the challenge and the puzzle of teaching children with ASD. But it's hard not to take it personally sometimes and to feel that the rough days are evidence that I don't know enough to have taken on this new class. Yet I know that the other staff and the children are depending on me.

So I leave school discouraged and disheartened but later that evening when I am finishing the dinner dishes, an idea comes to me. The next morning I arrive at school early and get to work on implementing the new plan. I set the three cube chairs in a row on the rug with a space of about eight inches between each one. Then I take masking tape and make a square on the rug around the perimeter of each so the chair fits exactly inside a tape border. Next I print the three boys' names on bright yellow paper and tape a name on the rug just behind each chair. Teddy will be in the middle, Luis in yellow to his right and James in the red chair to his left. Then we wait!

James comes over to the rug first after hanging up his coat. He reads each of the three names out loud and then settles down quietly in the red chair in front of his name. Soon the other two boys follow, Luis into his yellow chair and Teddy in the middle. The teachers all smile at each other at this sight but know enough not to assume this peaceful moment will last.

We begin with the morning greeting song and then move on to song choices. James stands up to take his turn to choose a song card and then returns to his red chair. He begins to work carefully to line his chair up again exactly inside the tape, correcting a slight shift that occurred when he stood up. Instead of constantly bumping his chair against the next one to get them in a straight line, his attention is now focused on being sure the red chair is perfectly aligned with the tape.

My hunch has paid off! Visual supports are often recommended to help children with autism follow a routine or complete a task. Giving James a visual boundary for his chair has changed the dynamic. Not a word is said but the visual cue claims his attention.

Of course soon after the first song is over, a young woman arrives who is making a video of our program for a workshop. She wants to capture morning circle and I soon realize she will have the best angle from the corner behind me.

But once she raises her camera she says quietly, "They're too close. Can you move them back a little?"

"Well, I can try," I say, looking at the new tape squares on the rug. Without saying anything, I push each chair back about six inches.

"No way," James protests at once, looking down and seeing that his chair is now off the line of tape in front and on the sides. He quickly scoots his chair until it is back inside the tape square. Teddy and Luis immediately follow suit.

"It's a long story," I say to the woman behind the video camera, "but that's as good as it is going to get."

"Well, Did You Do It?"

I'm reviewing a videotape we're making for a conference later this month, when I notice things I missed at the time. It's still rough footage so scenes alternate with wild shots that make you feel the room is spinning.

In one scene, the camera focuses on the three boys working independently – each one at the table designated as his place for the "work alone" segment of the day. This is a time for them to practice tasks we know they have mastered so they learn to work independently – a skill that will serve them well as they move on into higher grades. The work boxes are set out to their left with a strip of pictures in front of them. They match each picture to one of the boxes as they follow this visual work schedule.

The boys are arranged at the tables so they face in different directions to cut down on visual distraction. But watching the video I hear Luis begin to count in unison when Teddy is doing a counting task at his table.

Later Teddy pulls his second box forward and finds a lacing task inside.

"I can't do that," he announces when he sees it. He repeats his protest several more times until Maria stops by his table and says quietly, "You can do it, Teddy."

"I can't do that," he says one more time a few minutes later and then takes the animal shape out of the basket and begins to awkwardly push the thread through the first hole.

Meanwhile James has been working at another table with his back to Teddy. Captured on the video, he unzips a small plastic bag, takes out a thick rubber band and stretches it with both hands trying to fit it on the plastic pegs of a geoboard. The rubber band snaps away from him and lands on the table. He picks up the rubber band again, pulls it out and this time manages to hold it down and catch the pegs to attach it horizontally across the plastic board.

Without turning around, he calls out to Teddy. "Well, can you do it or can you do it not?"

There is no answer from Teddy as the video shows him busily putting his last workbox in the "all done" box, getting ready to leave his table.

James' voice is heard again. "Well, can you do it or can you do it not?"

By the third time James asks this in exactly the same way, Teddy realizes the question is meant for him. "I already did it," he says quietly.

"Well … that's all the best every anyway," James says, and that is apparently all he has to say about that. He continues to stretch the rubber bands on to the geoboard in front of him.

Teddy Works on Sad

Teddy has found his own way to work on his fear of being sad. His favorite way to introduce the theme is to say to Maria or Lilly, "You've lost your mittens." This is their cue that they are supposed to pretend to cry.

"Put your hands up like this," Teddy says the first time he invents this game and Lilly imitates his balled fists as she rubs her eyes, scrunches up her face and emits "boo hoo" sounds.

Teddy springs into action. "I will get you a tissue," he calls as he heads across the room in search of the nearest box of tissues. Once he has one in hand, he runs back to Lilly.

"Here you are you naughty kitten. You are sad," he says gently patting her on the back. Lilly wipes her eyes, sets the tissue aside and gives Teddy a big smile.

"I feel much better now," she says.

Sometimes that's enough and they move on to another game. But at other times Teddy begins the whole sequence again by calling out loudly, "You lost your mittens!"

Lilly soon learns that is her cue to burst into pretend tears again so they can rerun the entire scene.

"I played the sad game," Teddy tells me one day while Lilly is busy helping James in another part of the room.

"I notice you really like to play that game," I reply and with a quick nod of his head Teddy runs off to play at the water table.

I remember our introduction to Teddy's discomfort or fear of "getting sad" when Maria tried to have him say "*juice*" instead of "*goose*" at snack time. Since then we have been using sad events that occur over the course of most days to guide him through experiencing sad times. But now Teddy has taken charge and is creating his own play therapy with the recurring theme of the three little kittens.

Teddy's themes expand after the day he accidentally drops the receiver from the phone in the play restaurant over into the block area where James is playing. As usual James is lining all the wild animals up in pairs as if they were marching onto Noah's ark. The sudden appearance of the disconnected phone receiver in his ordered animal play startles James and he reacts immediately.

"Hey, don't do that," he yells at Teddy in a loud, gruff voice. Instantly Teddy's face reddens and folds in on itself as he begins to sob.

"It's alright," I say, coming over and squatting down next to Teddy. "James sounds very mad because that phone scared him."

Then I shift my focus to James and try to calm him down. "It's alright, James. That was an accident. Teddy didn't mean to drop the phone on your animals. Look at how Teddy feels."

Hoping he can get a bit of a grip on the situation, I direct Teddy, "Use your words to tell James how you feel".

He works hard to slow down his crying and then surprises me with the clarity and volume of his response. "James, I don't like it when you yell at me!"

"Well, don't do that," James says in a slightly gentler and quieter version of his protest - and so the mad game is born.

Maria is often the chosen partner for this game. "Don't be mad at me Maria," Teddy calls out when she joins him in the block area for guided playtime the next day. After a few missed boats we figure out that this is the cue that she is supposed to use a loud voice and say, "Don't do that Teddy" or "Don't knock down my building". There is more room for creativity in the mad game than in the repetitive script of the sad tale of the kittens and their lost mittens.

But the mad game requires that Maria use a stern voice and reprimand Teddy in a way that is similar to James' sudden anger at him. This then allows Teddy to look directly at Maria and announce in as strong a voice as possible, "Don't be mad at me, Maria. I don't like it."

Once he has done this, Teddy either starts the game all over again or signals he is done by going off to play in another area of the room.

* * *

At the end of music time a new routine has emerged in which each boy has a turn to play my guitar. This began one day when Teddy asked if he could play my guitar. I told him that he could do it later, after the three songs were finished. Like so many things with these boys, it has now taken on the quality of a ritual.

Today James is first to have his turn to sit in front and strum the guitar. James is the one who is most likely to actually sing as he strums. He begins to sing his version of Old MacDonald, loud and clear. Luis' attention is immediately captured and he watches carefully. James sings the opening lines and then pauses after the words "and on the farm he had a ……"

Luis understands this opening and happily supplies the name of an animal. "Cow," he announces and James takes his idea up and sings about the cow. James goes on with verse after verse, always pausing for Luis to fill in the blank and supply the name of the next animal. Each verse ends with James' abbreviated version of the phrases, but the boys are all happy with this. The only protest comes if Luis suggests an animal like a lion or a Care Bear. James immediately stops and refuses to go on until Luis names a farm animal.

At the end of Old MacDonald, James begins strumming a tune without words, reluctant to give up his turn with the guitar.

"Hey, sing some blues," Teddy calls out to James. Then he turns sideways in his chair, throws his long legs over the side of the cube and says to me, "Blues – that's about suffering."

I wonder where Teddy has picked up this information. I know that his parents follow the local music scene and sometimes take Teddy along to performances. James plays on and I don't want to interrupt Teddy's attention but I make a mental note to ask him more about suffering at a better time.

Five Green Speckled Frogs

I wonder later the next morning if it is a mistake to call attention to how Teddy is feeling and if I never should have mentioned that he is looking sad. As soon as the word "*sad*" is out of my mouth Teddy's face collapses as huge tears begin to run down his reddening cheeks. At first he is so overwhelmed with his feelings, the suffering he mentioned yesterday, that he can't talk at all. Luis and James both turn to look at him as he sits in the blue cube chair between them.

"Teddy sad," Luis says turning his own mouth downward as he thrusts out his bottom lip and knits his brows in his most dramatic depiction of sad.

"Yes, Teddy is sad," I say. Now James stands directly in front of the weeping Teddy and asks, "What's wrong, Teddy?"

Teddy takes a half breath and says haltingly, "I wanted to put the frogs away by myself."

Just moments before we'd finished singing the song about Five Green and Speckled Frogs. At the beginning each boy had helped attach the little cloth frogs to a mitt I held on my hand during the song. Then they took turns pulling a frog off at the appropriate point in each verse and throwing it into an imagined pool on the rug.

The problem comes at the end of the song when James jumps up and gathers all the frogs from the pond, stuffing them into the mitt to put them away. Teddy does not get a turn and that is why he is looking a little sad until I mention it and then he is VERY sad. He is completely carried away by his sadness.

It would seem simple enough to just retrieve a frog or two from the mitt and let Teddy put them away by himself and then move on to work time. But the mitt with all the frogs securely inside is in the firm double-handed grip of James. James is not at all sure what is up but he is quite sure he doesn't want to give anything to Teddy just then. So he reverts to one of his favorite lines for difficult situations. Pointing right at Teddy he declares in his medium loud voice, "Now you are really fired!"

To his credit, Teddy rises to the challenge, takes a deep breath and says in a more assertive than usual voice, "Don't scream at me James. I don't like it when you scream at me."

After some quiet but persistent negotiation, James is persuaded to pull two frogs out of the mitt and give them to Teddy. With a relieved smile on his face Teddy immediately puts them right back in the mitt – all by himself.

"Don't be mad at me James," he says, working in real life with the same line he uses in "the mad game."

James responds by putting the mitt with all the frogs inside back on the shelf near the window. Then he turns to Teddy again and announces, "That's it. It's over."

"Look at his face, Teddy," I coach pointing to James. "See – he is not mad anymore. James said, 'It's over.' That means he is not mad anymore."

I don't think Teddy is convinced of this but it's enough to help him get unstuck and allow us to move on to 1:1 work time with each boy going to work at his own table.

Later that morning after snack time, Teddy goes to the easel and draws a big circle in purple on the blank paper. With his right hand he draws one eye on the right side. Rather than crossing the midline, he switches the marker to his left hand to make the left eye and puts a small dot for a nose in the middle. Then using one hand and then the other, he draws a line with a definite upward turn at both ends for the mouth.

"Should I write your story about the picture?" I ask, squatting down beside him as he finishes the drawing.

"He is happy," he says and I print those words under his picture. "He likes to play with his friend James."

James was right, I think, it's over.

The Race to Be First Begins

Yesterday was the honeymoon – the first day back after the December vacation. Both James and Luis were excited to be back in school and hurried down the hall after I met their vans. They had greeted each other by name outside and then started off down the hall together. They came through the door to our room at the same time, quickly peeled off their jackets, stuffed them in their cubbies and ran over to their picture schedules.

Before I even had my jacket off, they put their music cards up on the easel and had both settled in their favorite chair on the rug. When Teddy appeared at the door a few moments later, they both rushed over to greet him with such intensity that Teddy was caught by surprise.

By the time I could get over to say hello to him, his lip was quivering and tears were running down his cheeks. "They…they scared me," he said overwhelmed by their energy or perhaps sensing their competitive drive to be the first to greet him. Once Teddy was reassured of their friendly intentions, he joined us at the rug and the morning went very smoothly.

But today is the second day back and the honeymoon is over. It begins when the automatic sensor turns off the lights in our room while we are all at the other end of the room for circle time. This is not an unusual occurrence. As soon as it happens, Luis runs across the room and waves his arms below the sensor until the lights come back on. With that James begins his first tantrum of the morning. He races over toward Luis yelling, "No…no Luis, that is not your time."

Seeing the lights come back on, James bursts into loud sobs. He comes back over to the rug and stands with his head bent over the empty blue cube chair where he had been sitting. As the tears drip off his cheeks, he watches them pool on the seat of his chair. From time to time he bellows a single word. As the pool of tears grows on the blue chair, Teddy's attention focuses on the puddle.

"Why is James sad?" he asks several times. Then he runs over and pulls two Kleenex out of a box, moving toward the blue chair to clean it off.

But Maria is there first. "Give them to James," she says quietly. "He can clean it up." Teddy holds the tissues out to his tearful friend.

"I just want to be alone," James announces and marches over to sit in one of the small wooden rocking chairs by the bookshelf. With his back to us he rocks in silence, leaning forward so that a small puddle of his tears now forms on the linoleum in front of the little rocker. Watching the puddle of his own tears seems in some way to have a calming effect on James. We move on to the next song with Teddy and Luis, while James quietly rocks and watches the pool on the floor.

Later in the morning, I call to Luis to go over and blink the lights as the signal that it is almost time to put toys away. All I say is, "Luis, would you blink the lights for clean up?" It is exactly the wrong thing to say and saying it from halfway across the room makes it worse.

Distracted by my own wish to get the boys outside for some play time before lunch, I miss the problem my words will create. As soon as I speak, I know it's a colossal mistake. Luis races across the room to climb up on the base of the cubbies to reach the light switch. James lurches around the other side of the block shelf, yelling as he comes and makes a lunge to grab Luis' legs to pull him down from the cubbies.

"It's my turn to be first," James is yelling as he tries unsuccessfully to dislodge Luis. It is 11:00 on a Tuesday morning in January that could aptly be called "The day the race to be first begins." There have already been three instances of James having a dramatic response to Luis doing something first. Each time James leans over and watches his tears pool in the chair or on the linoleum floor.

And each time Teddy runs over with a box of tissues that he offers while asking, "James are you sad?" James is so completely focused on his tears that he doesn't respond.

By Wednesday morning we are determined to head trouble off before it starts. Thinking back over the two days before, we all realize that the problem usually begins on the walk in from the vans. We just hadn't noticed it at the time.

We decide to change our behavior in an attempt to de-escalate the situation. Today we are on high alert from the moment their vans begin arriving. Luis' van arrives first and he comes off easily and cheerfully, always a good sign for the day ahead. We greet him and then suggest, "Let's wait for James' van."

Seeing two other vans in line behind his, Luis goes to the first van and peers in the open sliding door. "Oh no – no James," he says and goes on to the next van proclaiming, "Try again." James is there, smiling out from underneath yet another baseball cap.

"I need to be first," James announces as the driver opens the sliding door on the side of the van.

I think of letting Ben, a child from another class who is seated next to the door come out of the van first – a completely logical move. But one look at the intensity on James' face and I decide that this is not the day to push it.

Luckily Ben hasn't joined the perpetual race James is on, so he sits with his legs tucked up as James moves past him, takes my right hand and crouches a little before jumping from the van on to the sidewalk.

"I was first," he says immediately.

"Yes, you were. What will Ben be?"

"Second," James said.

"And second is okay too, isn't it Ben," I add, hoping to begin to expand the options for James.

"It's okay," Ben says cheerfully as he comes out of the van.

"Well it is *not* okay for me," James says in a rare moment of reflection. "I only like to be first."

By then Teddy has arrived with his parents so we begin the walk to our classroom.

"Hold hands," we announce cheerily, having practiced this routine for some days now. Luis, James and Teddy all join hands and walk into the school, take the left turn to our wing of the building and move down the hall toward our room. James manages to lean ahead just a bit, pulling Teddy along on his right while Luis moves steadily along on his left. Like a racehorse, James' head crosses the invisible finish line seconds before Teddy and Luis. Neither of them notices, they are content that they've all arrived together today. But I suspect that in his intense little heart, James knows that he is first if only by a tilt of the head and a forward lean of his shoulder.

It's Okay to be Second

This morning James' van arrives last and that carries the potential for a rough start to our day. Luis and Teddy are already here, standing on the sidewalk looking across the traffic circle as the last maroon van comes into the school drive.

"Let's wait for James," I'd said a few minutes earlier, knowing that if we took them on into school, we would have a disaster in the making. James is still very stuck on the need to be first. So we are already at a disadvantage because his van has, in fact, arrived last. But we are right there waiting for him, Teddy waving as the van approaches.

I slide open the side door and see the tension in James' face as he realizes that both of the other boys are already at school ahead of him.

"It's your turn to get off your van first today," I announce as I open the van door. His driver, Carrie, leaves her seat to release James' seatbelt. He is holding a huge teddy bear dressed in a new ski hat and wool sweater, perfect for this sunny January morning. James' face relaxes with the news that he will be first to get off the van. Fortunately neither of his van mates seems to care about this so James has been first off almost every day in recent history. But we like to think that we are building up the foundations of James' tolerance for being second.

By mid-morning James has a meltdown because both Luis and Teddy arrived at the snack table before he did. After James has calmed down, I join him at a table where he is drawing. I begin to tell him a story about the event at snack, printing the words on lined paper as he watches.

Today Luis was first at snack. Teddy was second. I was so mad I did not eat snack today. I want to be first."

A social story written in the first person is a technique used to help children by proposing a resolution to a problem they are having. When it was done I added construction paper covers and wrote the title "James can be Second" on the front. By the end of the day, James had the story memorized. Whenever he came to the key line, the not so subliminal message, I would point to the line and James would read, "It's okay to be second." We made him a copy of the book to take home so that he could read it with his family.

As James moves to come off the van the next morning, I coach him to say, "Thanks for letting me be first, Ben." Then before he climbs down from the van, he looks into the back seat and sees Patricia waiting her turn.

"Patricia," James says, "It's your turn to be second. It's okay to be second." Then with his giant bear in one hand, he accepts the hand I hold out to him and jumps off the van. He greets his two friends by name and then strains for the forward position as we begin to walk into the school and down the hall to our classroom.

Soon we are seated at the rug for morning meeting time. After a brief protest, James accepts the fact that his name is not next to "Choose the first song" on the helper chart. Instead he is the "guitar helper" and accepts that role officiously.

But when I try to sing the good morning song to Maria first, he immediately begins to be uncomfortable.

"No – James is first. Maria is second."

Maria immediately senses the dramatic possibilities and screws up her face as if she is about to cry.

"I don't want to be second," she says. "I want to be first."

"It's okay, Maria," James says. "It's okay to be second."

Maria keeps the sad look on her face as James watches her closely.

"Be happy Maria," he says reaching with his fingers to pull up the corners of her mouth.

"That's okay," says Maria, relaxing her face into a smile. "I can be first tomorrow."

"Look," James says to Teddy and Luis, taking hold of her chin and turning her face in their direction. "She's okay now."

As Maria says later in the day after reading the social story with him, "Well I guess it's a start. James now believes it is okay for everyone else to be second."

"I Already Told You That": Working on Language

We are short a teacher assistant today so I am working with both James and Teddy during structured work time. After a fast paced counting activity with magnetic shapes and numbers, they move on to the second workbox for the day. There is one sheet of paper in the red plastic box.

"It's a question game," I say, taking the sheet of paper they hand to me. "Today you get to play the game together."

Because understanding and processing language is a major challenge for children with autism, we focus a great deal of attention on helping both Teddy and James learn how to correctly understand what people are asking them. They have been making steady progress, the result of Eliza's ingenuity in their speech/language therapy and many activities during our structured work times. We used a sequence of practice sessions beginning with the simplest question, "What is this?" Now they are both able to answer most *what* and *who* questions, so we are moving on.

But in the hurry to get ready this morning, I never got around to putting any stickers or peel off letters in the box with the questions sheet. I'd used them before with James to reward him for each correct answer. He quickly solves this problem by reaching into the recycle materials shelf behind him and taking out a page of surplus stickers. With each answer he peels off a sticker and puts it on his striped t-shirt. He also peels one off and hands it to Teddy every time he answers a question.

"What did you eat for breakfast, James?" I ask.

"Spaghetti," he says, peeling a blue ice cream cone sticker off and putting it on his chest.

"What did you eat for breakfast Teddy?" I ask turning to where he is waiting.

"Dinosaur toast and then I had a grapefruit," he says immediately.

"When did you eat breakfast, Teddy," I ask switching the question to see if he can process the new question.

"In the morning," he says and James gives the same answer when asked, helped by Teddy's response.

Now it's James' turn to be first and I up the ante with a harder question. "**Why** do you eat breakfast?'

"In the morning," James responds proudly and adds a blue cupcake sticker to his shirt. The rewards are in his hands so he peels one off each time oblivious to the fact that some of the answers are wrong. My lack of careful preparation has come back to haunt me.

I turn to the other side of the table. "Teddy, WHY do you eat breakfast?"

"Because we got the dinosaur toast at Trader Joe's."

Just then Lilly walks by our table on the way to get something from the cupboard. "Lilly, why do you eat breakfast?" I ask her as she stops by the table to greet the boys.

"Because I'm very hungry in the morning," she says, adding drama to her words with facial expressions.

"Are you sad?" Teddy asks, trying to figure out what her changing expressions mean.

"No, I was showing how hungry I felt," Lilly responds with a smile.

Given her modeling, I decide that it is worth trying the question again with the boys.

"*Why* do you eat breakfast, Teddy?"

He thinks for a minute and then says, "After the dinosaur toast, I eat the grapefruit."

In one last try, I turn to James who is concentrating on peeling off a blue sticker of a party hat. "*Why* do you eat breakfast," I ask him.

He looks up at me, gives me a look that suggests he is running out of patience with these questions and says, "I already told you that – in the morning."

Clearly there is more work to be done on *why* questions!

The Categories Game

We begin to introduce more language games as part of our morning circle time. Luis is more willing to work on language when he has the other two boys to engage his attention and his sense of competition. When we first introduce the categories game, James' interest is captured immediately. We begin by having the children name each photo card as I line them up in the chalk tray on the bulletin board in front of our circle. Soon photos of animals, food and toys form a line. Three baskets are on the floor in front and I explain that one is for animals, one for food and the other for toys. I put one picture in each basket to show them where each category belongs.

It is Teddy's turn first, and I tell him to find one animal and one food. He's up in a flash and picks cards from each category with ease. "A camel and a watermelon," he says, naming each one as he carefully places one in the basket for animals and the other in the food basket.

"Now it's Luis' turn," I say. "Find one *animal*."

"No – slide," he says and picks up the card with the colorful plastic slide on it. It's not clear to me if this is simply a mistake resulting from his lack of understanding the concept of categories or if it is also related to his general wish to control activities.

"Where does the slide go?" I ask, pointing to the three baskets, one for each category.

"Here," he says, putting it on top of the watermelon in the food basket.

James is on his feet at once calling out, "No, that's the food." He manages to move the slide to the toys basket in spite of Luis' protest. Soon all the pictures have been chosen one way or another and we are off to individual work sessions.

For weeks the categories game is a mystery to Luis. "Find something you eat," I say. He comes up to the board and picks the picture of a shirt. Later he chooses a tiger when I ask for food. As we keep working on this challenge day after day at his work time, it becomes clear to us that he doesn't understand the concept of categories at all so he picks the card that is most appealing to him. But by playing the game consistently and limiting the choices so that he has repeated success, Luis begins to understand the concept.

Several weeks after we first started this game, James is first to play at morning circle time. Because he has mastered the basics of the game, I challenge him by giving him three directions. "Pick one animal, one food and one thing you ride on." James is up before I finish and chooses one thing from each category, placing them carefully in the correct baskets.

Next it is Luis' turn so I give him a simpler direction. "Luis, pick one food and one animal."

First he repeats the direction while he stays in his yellow chair. Then Luis walks up to the chalk tray and says, "Ice cream and camel" as he chooses those two pictures. James immediately recognizes this as a major accomplishment for his friend.

"You did it!" James says, jumping up to come and stand next to him and watch over his shoulder to see if he puts each card in the right basket. Luis grins as he starts to put the ice cream picture in the basket for the animals. "Hey, try again," he says and sets the card in the food basket on top of donuts and a watermelon.

The Blue Superman Shirt

This afternoon we have exciting news to share with the class, so I ask Maria to bring the large easel over to the rug right after our opening song. When he sees the easel with the large pad of lined paper on it, Luis puts his hands out in front of him to sign the word "now." Using sign and voice he then proclaims, "Now it is time for Kids' News." The easel signals this routine language activity for him and he uses the words and signs we always use to focus the group's attention.

I write a lead sentence on the top of the blank paper. "In the bush in the courtyard, there is a nest." But instead of writing the words bush and nest, I draw pictures at those places in the sentence. Then we read the sentence together and I ask the class, "What do you think is in the nest?" as I add that sentence to our chart.

Cali's hand shoots up first. "I saw a big tree at my house," she says.

"What do you think is in *our* nest, Cali?"

"And the mothers and the baby crack," she adds.

"You mean the eggs crack," Sarah corrects her.

"Yes eggs," Cali says, quite pleased with her somewhat jumbled contribution to our discussion. So I write her idea on the chart - "Mother and the baby eggs."

"I think squirrels," says Hercules and I add squirrels to our list.

"My turn," says Luis, putting up his hand as he sits up straight in his yellow cube chair that is positioned as usual on top of the letter R on our oval rug.

"Luis, what do you think is in the nest?" I ask, responding quickly to his eagerness.

"Blue Superman," he says, pointing proudly to the brand new Superman shirt he is wearing today.

I try re-reading the simple sentence with the pictures of the bush and the nest. But it is not at all clear to him what we are talking about and his news is about his "blue Superman" shirt. So I draw a little picture of a blue shirt on our list too. I look closely at his shirt and add a yellow shield with the red S in the center.

Luis' shirt fascination began last Thursday when Davi arrived in the afternoon wearing a new blue Superman t-shirt. Luis was immediately drawn to that shirt.

"Superman" he said, standing right in front of Davi. Then pulling his arms out of his own long sleeved white shirt, he began to pull it over his head. Once he had his shirt off, he pointed to Davi's new blue shirt and said, "Luis' turn".

"That is Davi's shirt," I said, handing him his white shirt from where it had fallen on the floor.

"No thanks," he said politely, "Luis' turn….Superman."

"That's Davi's shirt," I said again. "No turns."

"Luis says, yes turns," he said, then adding "please" in the hopes that would do the trick.

How do you explain this to a child with a communication disorder? Yes we have worked and worked to teach you to ask, to share, and to say please. But this is the exception to all those rules. It is not customary to ask for a turn with another child's shirt. Finally he gave up and went on to play.

But when his mother came later, I had Luis show her Davi's shirt so she would understand if he talked about "blue Superman."

This morning when Luis arrived on the van he had on blue basketball shorts with a matching jacket zipped up to his chin. After he jumped down from the van he came closer to me and took my hand – an unusual thing for him to do when he first arrives.

I bent down until my face was level with his to welcome him with a first greeting. He leaned his face closer to mine, held one hand up to screen his lips and whispered one word into my ear, "Superman."

A few minutes later when the three boys had walked hand in hand to our room, Luis stood in front of his cubby, unzipped his jacket and turned around. "Ta Da," he said with a flourish as he revealed his own bright blue Superman shirt. For the rest of the morning he would not answer to his name. If we called him Luis, he would point to his shirt and say, "Superman," smiling up at us.

So it is no wonder that the news that is most compelling to Luis at afternoon circle is the announcement that he now has a Superman shirt too. He still has major gaps in his ability to process language so all of our discussion about the nest in the bush in the courtyard remains a mystery to him. What he knows from the easel and the heading at the top of the language chart is that this is the day to share *Kids' News*. It is very clear to him that the news he has been waiting all day to share is about his Superman shirt. The other children watch carefully as I add his words to our list and then draw a picture of the blue shirt with a red S in the center. It comes right after the mother bird, the cracking eggs, the baby birds and the squirrels.

"Try Again"

There was a moment when I could have arranged for James to be first off the van again. But on this cloudy April morning when I slide the van door open, Felicia is in the car seat nearest the door. She looks at me expectantly and asks, "Is it my turn to be first?"

I can see James already straining to get out of his car seat and push past her to come out first, but I decide not to engineer things to allow James to do that.

Instead I tell Felicia, "Yes, today it is your turn."

To make matters worse, Ben moves quickly to come out of the back seat before James can get over to the door, so now James will be third off the van. That realization sends him onto the floor where he scoots over, leaning against the far side of the van with his legs tucked up under him.

"Now you are really fired!" he says several times, his eyebrows knit together over his dark brown eyes. All of my attempts to assure him that it's okay to be third are falling on defiant ears. He leans forward as huge crocodile tears roll down his cheeks and fall onto the floor of the van.

When James finally leaves the van, it is by moving like a snake along the floor and coming out head first towards the sidewalk. As I reach down to catch his body and help him arrive safely, we hear someone calling his name.

As luck would have it, his best friend from the afternoon class, Lucy is walking by with her father wheeling her bright pink bike. The sight of Lucy and her little black and white dog is enough to help James shift out of his angry mood.

At the same time Maria has been helping Luis out of his van. When I turn to greet Luis, he is holding a very full paper shopping bag by the two handles, showing the contents to Maria. She takes one look, smiles and passes it on to Lilly. I hear Lilly's sudden laughter as she holds the bag out for me to see. Stuffed in the bag is the same black felt Batman cape that Luis wore most of the day yesterday. But now it is squeezed into the bag with a mask, gloves and a plastic chest protector.

"You better keep laughing. It already promises to be quite a day," I say to Lilly as we head toward our classroom, James leading our procession by six feet.

As soon as we are in the room, Luis reaches into the bag, takes out the cape and slips it over his head, letting it rest on the shoulders of his black shirt with the silver Batman insignia. Next he takes out the chest protector and mask and is angry when Lilly tells him that we will save those for later.

"First music time," Lilly says, "then work time."

Luis protests briefly but when we don't yield, he turns his attention to getting the long black gloves first on one hand and then the other.

"Time for music," Luis announces as he marches over to sit in his customary yellow chair. He's holding his heavy black cape out behind him as he walks. James and Teddy are already seated, watching Luis' dramatic approach. We sing the greeting to James first and then Teddy before I move to sit right in front of Luis.

"Luis' turn," I say as I hold my hands out to clap with his gloved hands as we sing his name.

Instead of beginning to sing, he gives me a steady look and says, "Try again."

I'm in the dark about what I am supposed to do but luckily Lilly figures it out and I see a smile spread across her face.

"Oh it's Batman's turn," Lilly announces, cluing me in before I make another mistake. With that Luis claps his gloved hands on mine as we all sing, "Hello Batman, Hello Batman, we're glad you're here today."

By mid-May I begin to realize that Luis is outgrowing us. The boy who arrived with a vocabulary of three words – No and Shut Up – is now using his expanding, though unique, language to negotiate with his friends and to persuade his teachers to let him choose the order for his work tasks.

He is ready to leave us – but it is not at all clear that we are ready to let him go. He is such an energetic and enthusiastic little fellow and we are all dreading not having him here when we come back in September. It has been exhausting at times and discouraging when a day was dominated by his anger and our inability to soothe him. But he has come so far in the time with us and we delight in his humor and his persistence at working to find a way to get what he wants. He and Lilly have an especially close bond and we are all easily won over by the smile that spreads across his face when a problem is solved.

He and James will both be going off to kindergarten – with my strong recommendation that they be in different classes next year. They have certainly had a dynamic relationship and there has been a great deal of social learning going on through thick and thin. But knowing how often they are in some kind of competition with each other that interrupts circle time and takes considerable teacher attention, it seems wise to separate them.

Although James is ready for kindergarten in many ways, it is hard to know how the "race for first" will play in a larger group of children. Of course there are still three months before September; a great deal can happen in that time. The race may be over! He has a stronger command of language now and his early literacy skills will be assets that will help him succeed in kindergarten. He'll have special education supports if he needs them, but we expect that he will be able to spend most of his time in the regular kindergarten class. His parents believe this class has made a huge difference for James, and they are excited about his moving on next year.

We're glad that he and Luis will both be staying at this school so we can sometimes look through our window to the hall, and see them walking to their kindergarten classes. In September they'll be on the other side of that window, but we're glad that we'll be able to keep an eye on them.

As some of our children get ready to move on, we begin to meet new prospects, children who may be candidates for our class next year. The first child we hear more and more about is an "in-house referral". Sarah has been attending Louise's preschool down the hall since she turned three last September. I've heard Louise talk about her and know that she has gone to several trainings to learn how to work with Sarah who is blind. It has become clear to everyone that Sarah needs more intensive intervention to help her move ahead, so she'll be joining our morning class next September and will return to Louise's class in the afternoon. It seems a good plan to us because she will be able to continue with peers she has been with this year. Time will tell whether it seems like a good plan to Sarah!

In late May I find a referral form in my mailbox one afternoon asking me to evaluate a child named Samuel who turns three next month and will be moving to our school district during the summer. He has been attending a child care center in a nearby town and they have had serious concerns about his development. Samuel was recently evaluated by a neurologist and given the diagnosis of autism, so he is a possible candidate for our program.

When we first meet Samuel he is carried into our room with his legs wrapped tightly around his mother's waist. His head is pressed into her shoulder with his curly blond hair obscuring his face. He is not about to let go of her and walk into the strange room by himself. I set some small trucks and locking blocks out on a low table and invite his mother to sit with him there. Lilly and I move farther away so that he can have time to settle into the classroom without strange adults bearing down on him. His mother talks to him quietly and soon he is sitting next to her in the little blue chair, watching as she builds a tunnel for the small cars. They stay for over an hour, and during that time I never hear Samuel talk. According to the reports I have read, he is beginning to use one and two word phrases, but none were in evidence during this first visit. It can be overwhelming to come into a strange school and be watched closely by people you have never met – no matter how well intentioned they may be.

The first week in June, we have a Team meeting with Samuel's mother and the Early Intervention staff that work with him at his childcare center. Everyone is in agreement that Samuel should be in the full day program here next September, attending the intensive program in the morning and then staying as the other children join us for the afternoon class. I stand outside the school and talk to his mother for a long time after the meeting is over. She's worried about sending Samuel to a new school but she is also quite desperate to have him in a program where people can help him. I reassure her as much as I can, watching as she holds Samuel on one hip and he leans over to gently caress her neck.

"He likes to rub my neck like that," she says, realizing I've noticed.

"He's being very gentle," I say. "It must make him feel safe to be so close to you."

"We've been through a lot together," she says and I remember the report the social worker read in the meeting.

We say good-bye and I assure her that I will make a home visit in early September before school begins. I walk back into the school, holding the file filled with paperwork that will secure Samuel a place at morning music circle when we gather after the summer. He has already begun to make a place for himself in my thoughts and I know that the empty spaces James and Luis will leave in our days – and our hearts – will not be empty for long.

Davi is Sad

Something is ending and Davi, one of the afternoon children, is sad. In his journal today he draws a picture of himself with a straight line for the mouth. At the bottom of the page, he prints the words, "Davi is sad."

I turn back to the picture he had drawn in his journal two weeks ago. A boy stands in the middle of the page with exactly five fingers on each hand and five toes on each foot. That boy's face holds an unmistakable smile. "Davi is happy," he carefully printed beside his picture that day.

"Why is Davi sad on this page?" I ask him, turning back to the newest picture.

"I don't know," he says, his habitual answer to all questions we ask him about feelings.

Later today it's Davi's turn to cut one more paper circle off the chain we have been using to count down to the last day of preschool.

"Only six more days left," he says as he reaches high to cut the seventh circle away. Davi is not smiling when he sits back down in his place on the rug.

Something is ending. Teddy, the human buffer zone, is not a buffer zone at all anymore. After several weeks of seeming withdrawn, tired or quiet, he has entered a new phase. He has decided to join the action. When James falls on the floor in defiance, Teddy falls down next to him. When James leaps up in the middle of a song to touch the letters on the song chart, Teddy is up a moment later doing the same thing. When Luis stands up in the middle of a song although all the other children stay sitting on the rug, Teddy stands up too. Then he does his own awkward little dance in imitation of Luis' rhythmic side to side motion.

Something is ending and Teddy refuses to sit down at his table when Maria asks him to settle in to work time.

"Maria was crabby," he tells me a few minutes later when I come over to help him begin to do his work. He is not afraid of her being mad anymore and his face does not collapse in on itself. Something is ending, but something is beginning here too – some stronger, surer, sense of himself.

The End of the Year Party

It's the last day of school and all the children's families are invited for a celebration in the afternoon. We've planned a program with the children singing favorite songs that they have been practicing for two weeks. At first they sang the songs sitting on the rug as usual. But then we practiced having the children stand on the other side of the alphabet rug facing out to where the "audience" will sit. We knew that all of them needed practice, but especially Luis. There was no way he would do this new thing unless we did it enough that it would feel familiar to him. Yesterday Lilly had the brilliant idea of turning the alphabet rug around so that Luis' usual place on the letter R is now on the side where we want him to stand for the performance.

Luis' mother Emily and his grandmother arrive a little early and are the first family to come. As soon as Luis sees them, he thinks it is time for school to be over for the day. He heads for his cubby to get his backpack, calling "Good-bye kids" back over his shoulder. We try to explain to him that his family is going to stay. At first he is determined that it is time to leave, that his mother has come to pick him up as she does sometimes.

Finally Emily thinks to use the word "party" and that gets his instant attention. He comes back over to the rug area, sits in his yellow chair and says to his friends, "Sing Happy Birthday Luis."

Soon other families arrive and take their places in the odd assortment of chairs we have arranged in rows. The children take their places on the rug facing their families – all the children except Luis. He is still sitting in the yellow cube chair in the front row of the seats we had arranged for the audience.

Most people have arrived by now so we begin the singing. Before we start, I tell Luis, "Time for music. Come here and sing."

He is calm and polite in his refusal. "No thanks, Marion," he says and remains in the front row.

We go ahead and begin and, sure enough, midway into the first chorus of "This Little Light of Mine", Luis comes up and joins the children who are now standing on the rug, singing and signing the song. The other children shift over just enough so Luis can be in his favorite place on the letter R facing the audience. As the first song ends, flash bulbs go off as parents take pictures of the group. Luis calls out "Cheese" and poses with a wide smile and one hand held out with his thumb up.

Before we can begin the next song we had planned, Luis calls out, "What are you wearing?'

"It's not a fashion question, it's a song request," I explain to the families gathered.

Lilly and Maria had both predicted that he would want to sing that song because we had played the game several times over the last week and Luis often stole the show with his antics and enthusiastic singing. So though it was not our plan, we add the song to the program.

In the middle of the song, Phillip's parents arrive a little late. Scanning the chairs lined up in the audience area, they see two chairs in the front row and quietly move to sit in the yellow chair and the one next to it.

As soon as the song is over, Luis points to Phillip's father. "Who's that?" he asks Lilly.

She leans over to Luis and whispers, "That's Phillip's Daddy."

Without leaving his place on the letter R, Luis points to where Phillip's father is sitting and says loudly, "Hey Phillip's Daddy - that Luis' chair."

It takes Phillip's father just a minute to understand he is being spoken to and then he respectfully moves to another chair, leaving Luis' yellow chair empty in the front row.

Only then can the program continue. In addition to the songs, we have promised a short puppet show today. We've been planning this for weeks as the children worked in groups of two or three to paint animal puppets for an Eric Carle story.

Although we have been rehearsing every day for two weeks, Luis still isn't clear what this is all about. The two screens we set on the rug area to mark our stage seem to him to be an invitation for roughhousing. He usually darts in and out, parting the little curtains as he dives through the screen to the other side.

At the beginning of each rehearsal the children were lined up on a row of chairs in the order their animal appeared in the play. Some found their places easily; others needed an adult to help them sit and then a cue for when to stand

Luis was not to be contained in any chair until today when, miraculously he rises to the occasion and sits in line with the other children. He doesn't sit silently but he is in the right place. As we read the lines for each child and their puppet to move across the stage, the narrative is punctuated by Luis calling out each child's name.

"Now Teddy," Luis announces as Teddy moves up to center stage holding the Red Wolf puppet carefully over his head.

"No talking," Teddy says in a stage whisper as he takes his place.

When it is his turn Luis accepts the Macaroni Penguin puppet presented to him and carries it across the stage to stand with the children. But when the puppet show is almost over, instead of staying with the other children for the final song, Luis walks straight ahead and sits down in his yellow chair. He sits in the front row proudly holding Macaroni Penguin up above his head, surrounded by mothers, fathers, brothers, sisters and family friends

The other children sing the final song, "Good-bye Dear Friends"; the grand finale for this group we've loved. I know if I look at Lilly or Maria they will be crying and then I will too. So I keep my eyes on the audience with Luis smiling back at me from his yellow chair in the front row.

Most of the children will be off to kindergarten. Luis and James will go on to different kindergarten classes with special education support as needed. Only Teddy will be in the cube chairs when we gather for music circle again in September. We already know of at least two other children who will join him but hope that he won't need to be a human buffer zone next year. There will be new personalities, new friendships, new challenges and new stories. With the children's help we trust we will keep on finding our way – one day at a time.

The Second Year

A New Year Begins

Summer is over and we're working to get the classroom ready for the new school year. Maria, Lilly and I have a few days before the children start, and we're busy setting the room up after the custodians have cleaned and waxed all the floors. We start each day with a long list of tasks as we get ready to welcome Teddy back and meet the new children who will come to our morning and afternoon classes.

This afternoon I walk over to visit Teddy at home before school starts. I'm eager to see him because he's been away much of the summer. His father greets me at the door and Teddy comes running down the stairs from his bedroom calling out to me, "Let it be, let it be, let it be." It isn't until his father fills in the gaps that I realize he is chanting the chorus of the Beatles song.

"When I find myself in times of trouble, Mother Mary comes to me," I sing back to him, standing in the hall to greet him.

But Teddy isn't interested in the verse; it's the chorus that has captured his attention. "No, no," he calls out in frustration. "Let it be, let it be, let it be. That is # 26 on my CD."

"That's the Beatles," I say. I look at him and see that his lips are moving but I can't catch the words. So I squat down to be closer and hear him whisper four names -"John, George, Paul and Ringo."

"He'll only whisper when he says their names," his mother says quietly. "We're not sure why."

"It's # 26," Teddy says speaking out loud now, "and only two are alive because two are buried in the cemetery in London town." With that he is back off to his room to listen to more of his CD.

"It's # 26," he calls back over his shoulder. "That's a 2 and a 6."

Over tea and scones in the kitchen, Teddy's parents fill me in on their summer travels and visits with family. We talk about Teddy's progress and their goals for him in the months ahead. They also mention to me that Teddy has recently developed a strong interest in dead end streets. No sooner have they told me this than Teddy appears again, carrying a large drawing pad with him.

"This is my maps," he says, setting the pad on the table in front of me as I move my tea cup and plate to the side to accommodate the large paper. Opening the front cover of the pad, he shows me a page filled with curving lines going here and there.

"It's a map," Teddy says. Pointing to one straight line that ends in the middle of the paper he says, "Paradise Road is a dead end street." Next to the line one of his parents has carefully printed the name of the street. Other curving lines also have street names next to them and I recognize that it is a rough map of his neighborhood.

"This is California where Grandmommy and Poppa live," Teddy says as he turns to another page with curving lines labeled with street names that are unfamiliar to me. Teddy recites most of the names as I point to them on his primitive map.

His parents tell me that their late summer afternoons often included a drive to explore new dead end streets in town on the way to or from an afternoon swim. Once again I am in awe of their creativity and patience in helping to use Teddy's interests as a springboard for learning. His maps have become a way for him to practice drawing skills and see the street names in print. They've used his fascination with dead end streets as a vehicle for readiness skills.

"Be prepared to talk with Teddy about dead end streets," I tell Lilly and Maria later when I go back to school. But in our rush to have all the toys and art supplies ready for school on Monday, I completely forget to tell them about Teddy's fascination with the Beatles.

Meeting Sarah

Today's the first day of the new school year and the routines of our small classroom are completely new to Sarah. Because many of the children in our program have serious language deficits, we use picture cards and visual cues extensively. At music time every day three picture cards are lined up on a choice board on the easel. Each child has a turn to choose a song by pulling off the picture card for the song they want and putting it on the small purple square with a single piece of Velcro in the center. This allows children who have little or no language to participate and make a choice.

But for Sarah we need new options. Blind since birth, picture cards are of no use to her. Instead we have gathered a bucket of objects, each one a symbol for one of our songs. A little school bus with brittle wheels falling off, a toy teapot, and a soft cloth duck all serve as cues for a song choice.

Today we put a little stuffed monkey and a plastic star on the small wicker tray and hold them out in front of Sarah. "Sarah," I say as I hand her the monkey, "Five Little Monkeys." Then I place the little star in her hands and say, "Twinkle Little Star."

Sarah's hands both close around the little yellow star and she begins to sing in a clear voice, "Twinkle, twinkle little star, how I wonder what you are." It is the first time I've heard Sarah's voice so clearly.

After lunch on the first day of school, the new afternoon children arrive and we begin with an opening circle that borders on chaos. Ten new preschoolers are eager to talk, responding to some phrase I must have used. They are all talking at the same time and showing me their shoes, though I have no idea what I said to trigger this response.

The only returning child is Teddy, left behind as the two powerhouses, James and Luis, have gone on to kindergarten. Teddy knows what is supposed to be happening. He knows it's time to choose the first song, so he's not talking about shoes. But he hasn't come up to the easel to pick one of the song cards as I've asked him. Instead he's still sitting in his place on the rug, calling out to me over the din of the shoe talk.

"Can we sing 'Let it Be'? Can we sing 'Let it Be'?" he says over and over, never pausing long enough to leave an opening for my answer.

When he calls out for that song again, I finally have to go over to him and say firmly, "No Teddy, we can't sing 'Let It Be' now, none of the other children know that song."

His bottom lip quivers. "I'm sad," he says but then he pulls himself together, comes up to the easel and chooses the picture card for "Wheels on the Bus".

"It's 'Wheels on the Bus'," he tells the other children in a loud voice. There is no need to whisper, this is not a song to inspire the same kind of awe as when he whispered the Beatles' names.

At the end of the day, on my way back from sending the new preschoolers home, Luis is coming down the hall with his mother on his way home from his first day of kindergarten. I'm talking with another teacher in the hall who he doesn't know, so he calls out to us with a greeting that he adapts to the situation.

"Hey, hello there guys," he calls out with a smile spreading across his face. His hair has grown long and shaggy over the summer in contrast to the severity of the shaved head he had last June. He's dressed in baggy shorts and a long T-shirt with his Nike backpack slung over his shoulders.

As we get closer he says to his mother, "This is Ms. Marion." He introduces me as if I'd never met his mother Emily before. I think of all the work that went into teaching him this social skill and remember the day he put the visitors from the Ukraine to the test, cuing them to say hello to all the children and teachers. Now he uses this hard earned social skill to introduce me to his mother as if for the first time.

"Can I give you a hug?" I ask and, when he says yes, I bend down and give him a loose hug.

"Who is your new teacher?" I ask him.

"R.V.," he says and when I look puzzled Emily explains that this is currently his favorite video. I decide to try another question but first I give him a clue as to the topic.

"David is in your class. Who are your friends at school?"

By now Luis has caught sight of his own reflection in the window of the therapy room and he is trying different postures.

"C.V.S." he answers after a minute.

"C.V.S. is a store," I respond. I give up on the topic of friends and try to engage him around the theme of a drug store. "I buy soap at C.V.S. What do you buy?"

Luis doesn't answer and then he takes his mother's hand and says cheerfully, "We gotta go." I remember that was the line he would use anytime she came in to the preschool class even if she'd planned to stay awhile.

"Good-bye," I call after him as he pulls his mother on down the hall. When he is about twenty feet away, he turns around, crooks the index finger on his right hand and calls out to me, "Be happy!" With that benediction, he heads home from his first day of kindergarten.

Dumbo and Dead End Streets

We soon learn that Teddy's current interests include Dumbo as well as dead end streets. All day yesterday when any new adult came into the classroom, he would rush across the room and say to them, "You have Dumbo?"

People weren't at all sure what he said and even those who understood each word couldn't make enough sense of the question to venture an answer. So we begin helping him shape this enthusiasm into a coherent sentence.

"Say 'Did you see *Dumbo*?'" we cue him and this works better. Jen, a speech/language therapist, answers at once that she loved that movie when she was a little girl Teddy's age.

"How old are you?" Teddy asks her next.

"Thirty," Jen says. "Frio," Teddy announces. We are all puzzled.

"Frio?" Jen asks.

Then Maria decodes it. "You're right," she says to Teddy. "Thirty is a three and a zero."

"I can't say that hard sound - firty," he says as he heads over to the block area to find his favorite wooden truck.

"Say Dumbo," Teddy says to the school secretary when she comes into our room later to deliver some forms we need. I am close enough to them to interrupt before she can say the word.

"Wait, Teddy," I say, "First you have to say hello to Mrs. Dempsey."

"Hello Mrs. Dempsey," he says quickly. "Do you see *Dumbo*?"

"A long, long time ago and I liked it," she answers. "Do you like that movie Teddy?"

"Yes," he says excitedly and then the line he has been waiting for. "Say Dumbo!" Mrs. Dempsey pauses, smiles and says a very clear and emphatic, "Dumbo."

With that Teddy is off, his objective achieved, content with whatever special pleasure he gets from hearing people say his current favorite word.

Meltdowns in the Hall

The walk from the front door of the school through the crowded and noisy front hall to the relative calm of our classroom is usually a difficult time for Sarah. That means it is also a difficult time for the adult who is coaching and encouraging her along the way. The noise and confusion of other children and adults suddenly coming up behind her seems to set her on edge. She often ends up sitting down on the floor, crying and protesting loudly by repeating a phrase the adult has unwittingly provided as a trigger for her echolalic behavior.

It's Monday morning and I've been delayed by a phone call so it is a little late when I am heading to the front door to meet the children arriving on the vans. I hear Sarah's voice before I can see her. "No cane, no cane," she is saying when I come around the corner and see her sitting down in the hall just outside the cafeteria, her long dark hair pulled into a ponytail that dances from side to side with the repetitive motion of her head.

Lilly has Sarah's backpack over her shoulder and she's holding Sarah's light blue jacket in one hand and her short white cane in the other. Seeing me round the corner she shifts the jacket to the same hand as the cane so she can lift one finger to her lips, signaling that I should ignore the protests and not speak to Sarah until she's quiet.

A minute later Sarah quiets down long enough to take a deep breath. In that lull, I have time to squat down next to her and say quietly, "Good morning Sarah." These three words are all it takes for her to recognize my voice and she reaches a hand toward me as she says, "Hi Miss Marion."

I take hold of her hand and that is enough of a cue for her to stand up again. Fortunately the kindergarten classes have gone by already and the hall is quieter now.

"Want to play the piano?" I ask.

"Play the piano," she repeats as she starts to walk. I hold her cane out in front of her, and putting my hand over hers, position our hands on the top of the cane without naming it or giving a verbal direction to hold the cane.

"Play the piano," she says again as she walks along beside me and I help her hold the cane in a diagonal position across the front of her body.

I remember the first time I went to Sarah's home just before she was to begin in our class this year. I watched her move by herself from the toy box on one side of the living room to the piano where her father sat playing one note at a time.

I had only seen her in the regular preschool class down the hall where she spent the last school year. I had never seen her move independently from one place in the room to another. That was one of the things that concerned us – her lack of initiative in exploring the classroom environment.

"That's not at all like the other children I've worked with," the vision specialist has said to us. "Most blind children crawl around and reach out to touch things to explore and investigate, but not Sarah."

But when her father sat down and played those notes on the piano, she stood up on her own and walking sideways, stepping one foot out and bringing the other up beside it, she made her way alone from the box of toys over to the piano bench. Climbing up, she reached her small hands out and one note at a time, played the melody of 'Twinkle, Twinkle Little Star."

The Puzzle Named Samuel

It's only the second week of school and Samuel has surprised us with more language than we had expected. When Teddy gets stuck in one of his loud, laughing spells, Samuel looks over at him at the snack table and says, "That's not funny."

One afternoon as Samuel watches Jennifer, one of the afternoon children, move up the playground climber near him, he looks up at her and twice asks "What's your name?" until she finally answers.

But when his empty paper cup falls off the table at snack time, he falls to the floor crying and kicking. When a puzzle piece doesn't fit right the first time, he slides out of his chair under the table and begins to scream.

We begin to chart these incidents to try to identify what triggers them and to use this data to help us plan our intervention. The chart fills up the first day and we begin to see a pattern. When anything starts to go wrong, Samuel has only one response: cry and fall on the floor.

We try to be alert to the first signs of something going awry and come in quickly with a cue to Samuel to ask for help. One time yesterday as a puzzle piece turned frustrating and he was on the verge of falling off his chair, Lilly said, "Say 'Say help me.'"

As he did, she quickly turned the puzzle piece so that he could easily push it in.

Two more pieces fit easily and then another was turned wrong in his hand. Before Lilly said anything he asked on his own. "Hep me," he said and another outburst was headed off at the pass. But other tantrums are on us before we see them coming. There he is down on the floor somewhere in the classroom, kicking and crying.

Ever since school began this year, we've been struggling with how to respond to Samuel's sudden tantrums and Sarah's meltdowns in the hall. Because both are behaviors we want to decrease and eventually eliminate, we want to be careful not to reinforce them by paying attention to them. Planned ignoring is an important tool in promoting behavioral change but it is not easy, especially when the child is doing something loud or disruptive. It is much easier to ignore some of Teddy's silly behaviors than the outbursts of the other two children.

One evening when I go to my weekly writing group, I spend the time writing a memo to the staff that I call "Thoughts on Ignoring."

Thoughts on Ignoring

Part 1: Things to Ignore

1. Ignore Samuel when he falls to the floor crying and kicking – or even screaming. Ignore as in do not talk to him, do not explain or attempt to reason, and do not even make eye contact. If possible, remove yourself from the immediate area as long as he is safe.

2. Ignore Sarah when she sits down in the hall on the way from the playground or to the playground or back to lunch. Treat her behavior as if she is asking for a break. Give her words for this by stating, "I want a break" or "Take a break". Then set the cow-shaped timer for 1-2 minutes and say nothing else to her. You have the advantage that she can't see you so you don't need to move away, just keep quiet. After a bit if she has calmed down, make the timer ring and say brightly, "Break all done" or "All done break". Either order will work or not depending on factors that remain a mystery to us, our turn to be blind. In a pinch, if you do not happen to have the timer with you, resort to becoming a human timer. Eliza, our creative speech therapist, tried this and it worked at least once. She just said "ding" and then told Sarah to stand up.

3. Ignore Teddy when he laughs over and over even after Samuel has declared, "That's not funny!" This may mean moving away from him during music circle and sitting at the other

side of the small group. Also ignore repetitive comments like "Tickle, tickle, tickle" and comments that end in the word "hotel" like "Dumbo hotel" or "Stop and Shop Hotel" or "hummus hotel".

Part II: Things Not to Ignore

1. Do not ignore Samuel when he is able to say, "Hey, hep me" when a puzzle piece does not fit or the small horse has fallen out of sight between his work table and the shelf placed there to create a closed space for him. Respond immediately or sooner to any appropriate request while also saying "Good job talking!" or some variation of that. Failure to do this will quickly bring you back to Part 1, #1 – "Ignore Samuel when he falls to the floor crying and kicking…."

2. Do not ignore Sarah when you suddenly hear a spontaneous request in the midst of her musical phrases and echolalic lines. Immediately focus on the request. When she says "everybody" after you have asked what is next, understand that she means, "Sing *'I'm so glad everybody's here today'*." Jump on it – sing it with her, hold her hands up in excitement and make that communication work to get her something she wants. That's what it is all about!

    Failure to do this will be a missed opportunity and she will begin to slap the back of her hands against her mouth and Teddy will come running across the room and ask "Why is she sad? What is she doing?" That can be a very hard question to answer. So it is okay to admit to Teddy that sometimes we don't know what Sarah wants but that we are working to figure it out.

3. Do not ignore Teddy when he is in the play restaurant area and tells you to put the little apron on your head and tie it under your chin. The drape of the apron when worn on your head does look a little like Dumbo's big ears and that is funny and worthy of his laugh. Next he will serve you a piece of plastic cheese on rubber white bread and say, "Now Dumbo, here is a sandwich". Then he will say "Take it off" and you

can untie the apron and put it back on the shelf until the next time he asks. That may be right away or it may not be until another day. He will let you know when it is time.

Sarah Invents a Game

Sarah invented a new game today, an accidental breakthrough during her request for a break during her work time. The request was a major triumph in itself after several days of Sarah's resisting all of our efforts to engage her in the activities we had planned. It may be that she's having a hard time giving up the freedom of the summer months, an understandable reaction to the return of more structure and demands in her daily life. I've been having some of the same resistance myself to coming back to the routines of work after summer days for reading, swimming, riding my bike and visiting with family.

Wednesday Sarah shook her head back and forth adamantly saying "no, no, no" over and over again when we presented the shape sorter and then a new matching game with textured cylinders. I think she will like this new challenge eventually but today she was resisting doing anything I presented during work time. It is my first day this week to work with her during the intensive teaching time, so I am trying to find some way to move her beyond her pattern of refusals.

"Do you want a break on the bed?" I'd asked earlier in the session and she responded to that idea with the same pattern of headshakes and "no, no, no." I was getting discouraged.

As I reach over to the shelf to set one more new thing on the table to try to break the cycle of refusals, Sarah suddenly announces. "Want a break on the bed? Yes I do."

"Find the bed," I respond quickly and she stands up and moves away from the table. Holding one arm out in front of her, she makes her way across the three feet of rug that separate her from the mattress we use as a couch in the library area. Her hand touches the mattress and Sara climbs up onto the bed, snuggling down into the pillows with a satisfied expression on her face.

I watch her relax as she feels the pillows all around her. I sit down beside her and put one pillow over her legs. "Sarah is hiding," I say as I put another pillow loosely covering her torso and head.

"Where's Sarah?" I call out and, after a moment, Sarah reaches one hand out to pat the top pillow before pushing all the pillows off onto the floor. I laugh and give her several gentle bounces on the bed as I exclaim in a teasing voice, "I found you."

With that the hiding game is born and my job is to introduce more reciprocity and language into the game. Because Sarah tends to echo exactly what is said, she is soon repeating all my lines. "Where's Sarah," she says after I put the pillows on, and then once she has thrown the pillows off she announces, "I found you."

The challenge for me is to build language patterns that will sound more natural and therefore will be functional. But there's no doubt I have her attention and she is engaged in something she wants to keep doing. The refusals are over and Sarah laughs as I add more sensory input with gentle pressure and bounces with the pillows.

"Do you want to play hide again?" I ask. Sarah responds after a short pause, "Do you want to play hide again? Say yes I do." I realize that she is saying my lines and hers again so I try to teach it a different way.

"I want to play hide," I say the next time. Sarah takes this new sentence and adds it on to the string she's already memorized. "Do you want to play hide again? Say yes I do. I want to play hide."

Fortunately Eliza, our speech therapist, arrives just in time to help model a better way to do this. She strips the request down to the words we want Sarah to use to make a more natural sounding request. "Want to play hide again?" she asks, minimizing the intonation pattern that indicates a question. If Sarah will repeat this phrase be a more natural request.

At first Sarah still uses the full string of question, answer, statement that she had learned with me. "Do you want to hide? Say yes I do. I want to hide again."

Eliza ignores all the extra words, pauses and then makes the simple statement, 'I want to play hide again."

When Sarah repeats that one phrase, Eliza immediately puts a pillow on to hide her, jiggling her up and down on the bed and making the game as much fun as possible. Over and over as Sarah asks for the hiding game, Eliza varies her responses and adds more language to help Sarah practice more spontaneous requests.

After two days of constant refusals during work time, we have finally found something that engages and delights Sarah. I write a note to her parents in her notebook telling them about the hiding game so they will understand what she is asking for if she takes this request home with her for the weekend. All our carefully planned activities will still be there waiting on the little shelf next to her table when we come back next week. But for now, the hiding game moved Sarah beyond all her refusals and we've found something she asks to do over and over again.

"Now What Should I Do?"

On this dark, rainy September day, Jonah arrives for the afternoon class wearing a green raincoat and bright orange boots. He comes into the classroom with his mother and doesn't say a word to anyone. That is the heart of the problem. He can talk – he does talk at home - but he spent all last year in another preschool program and almost never spoke. He also never ate snack at his other school and so far that is true here too. Jonah has come to be part of our afternoon class of eleven children this year in the hope that we can figure out what is going on for him and then do something about it.

Today, as he has every day, he enters without greeting anyone and stands near his cubby looking around the classroom. His straight brown hair falls in bangs across his forehead and he watches the other children as they move toward the rug for music time, talking to each other as they go.

His bright blue eyes turn down to look at the floor as Lilly greets him. She talks quietly, commenting that his orange boots are perfect for a rainy day. She is careful not to ask him a direct question because then he will be put on the spot, expected to speak. He won't speak and that will be another experience of failure or holding out or of the power of silence. We can't figure it out yet so for now we take the course of waiting.

Later when no one is focusing attention on him, when there is not a direct question he's expected to answer, he moves over to join the class discussion about a field trip we will take to the fire station next week. We are making a list of things the children think we might see and his classmates have named fire trucks, ladders, fire helmets, hoses, and a fire dog. I print all these ideas on a chart as the children talk.

Then I hear Jonah asking a question. "Will we get buoy – ned?" he asks. He has to repeat his question two more times as we try to understand the last word. Finally we figure out that he is asking, "Will we get burned?"

"Oh no," I assure him, "there is no fire at the fire station." I wonder what picture he has in his mind that led to the question and what other fears might be hiding behind his silence.

I haven't heard Jonah join in any of our songs yet, though he will choose a song by picking one of the picture cards. He never participates in movement activities or copies the hand motions of other children during our songs.

I'm puzzled about this and wonder if he has trouble with the motor planning involved in motor imitation. Or is he just shy and uncomfortable with movement "on demand?"

I decide to try to figure this out later as everyone else is finishing snack. When Jonah is cleaning up the place where he sits without objection but never eats, I say, "Come with me for a minute; I want to teach you a game."

We go out in front of the window between the classroom and the hall. I give him his choice of cube chairs lined up there and then I settle in another chair that I pull up so we are facing each other.

"We're going to play the copycat game. You should try to copy everything I do but I think I might be able to trick you," I said, having learned that he often responds to the idea that he is tricking someone.

I clap my hands, stamp my feet and then hold my arms in different positions. Jonah quickly and effortlessly matchs everything I do. Soon we are jumping and twirling in the hall as he takes his turn to be the leader and I have to follow him. I knock on the window to let Lilly and Maria watch this unfolding evidence that the issue, whatever it is, is *not* motor planning.

When we go back in the room I invite three other children to join Jonah in the copycat game so we can see if he will also do this with a few other children. We draw five little chairs into a circle on the rug – four children and me. First I'm the leader and the children match all of my actions, Jonah never missing a beat until I stand up and he stays firmly planted in his chair.

Then I tell him that it is his turn to be the leader and I trade chairs with him. He comes right up to the front and begins– first hands on his knees, then on his toes and on and on. Jonah pulls his corduroy pants up to show his bare shins, laughing out loud as he sees us all follow him in this silliness. The more the children laugh, the higher he pulls his pant legs up until his bare knees are showing. We all follow as best we can and Jonah laughs out loud at the sight. But when it is his turn to pick the next child, he won't speak. That is another thing he will not do – call another child by their name. After a long pause he finally points to Kelly and she comes up to the front and takes his place as the leader.

Later in the afternoon Jonah is still drawing in his journal long after the three other children in his small group have finished their drawings, dictated their story and gone on to free play time. He is very methodically drawing lines from the left side of the page to the right. He is using a purple marker now but the entire bottom half of the paper is covered with blue lines, each one about one quarter of an inch above the one before. He has been moving his way up from the bottom of the page. The lines are not straight but have a wavy quality with each one following the route of the one before. On the blank page opposite, Lilly has printed his description of the work in progress. "It is a kind of balloon."

All this time Jonah has been making the lines of his balloon, oblivious to the fact that all the others have left his small group table and gone on to free play. He would probably still be drawing in blue but Lilly finally told him, "Now it's time for another color."

So he moves on to red after purple and then on to green, working on up the paper until black lines finish the pattern. He doesn't stop until he reaches the top of the page and there is no more space for another wavy line.

He just sits there now looking at his picture and glancing around the room where everyone else is busy in the activity of their choice during free play time. Lilly goes over and sits down next to him.

"Where do you want to play today, Jonah?" she asks.

"I don't know," he answers tentatively. "What *should* I do?"

"This is your time to choose. You can do anything you want now, Jonah. This is called free play time. What do you want to do?"

Jonah fiddles with the markers that are still on the table and then looks up at Lilly. "What do you think I should do?" he asks her.

Sensing his distress, Lilly helps him out, looking around the room as she names the places where children are already busy.

"You could go to water table, or painting or blocks. You could go to play in the house with Teddy or you could go over and read a book with Jennifer."

"But what *should* I do," Jonah asks again.

"Let's go read a book with Jennifer," Lilly suggests, realizing that right now it's too much for him to choose from all the possibilities.

"We should go and read a book," Jonah answers her and putting the markers back in the basket on the table, he heads over to sit on one end of the mattress that serves as our couch, as far as he can be from Jennifer. But as soon as he sits down she greets him and moves over to sit right next to him, her blond hair pulled into two slightly askew pony tails.

"Oh hi, Jonah, you can share my book," she says, her friendly spirit a strength that we hope will help her cope with all the challenges that she faces in learning readiness skills.

Jonah doesn't say a word but he does hold one side of the book she sets into his lap and turns back to the first page so Lilly can begin to read.

Teddy and the S Word

Teddy won't tell me what the word is at first because he is trying so hard *not* to say it. "It's the S word. I am not supposed to say the S word," he says when he runs up to me early on this Monday morning as we are waiting outside the school for the children to arrive. His mother sees my puzzled look and says quietly, "There's a note in his book that explains this. I don't want to say it right now."

So we go on to the playground and while Teddy and Samuel are crawling through the tunnel, I pull his home/school notebook out of his backpack, curious to see what this is all about. His mother wrote that sometime over the weekend Teddy began to use the word "stupid" in a variety of contexts. His parents tried hard to ignore this but found it harder and harder to do. They suggested other words he could use instead– silly, surprising, outrageous. But none caught on and he often went back to calling something or someone stupid. Finally they made a rule that he could not use the "S word" because it's a word that hurts people's feelings.

Teddy is trying very hard not to say the word when he greets me today. Later, walking in from the playground, the two of us are out ahead of the others and he stops to look down the storm grate that always draws his attention. After dropping a leaf down into the shallow water below, he starts to walk on toward the school door.

"Stupid is not a good word to say," he says.

"You're right," I agree. "That is not a kind word. It makes people sad."

All morning when any other adult enters our classroom, he sees his opportunity. He rushes over to stand near them and as soon as they make eye contact he says, "Stupid is not a good word to say!"

If he's lucky they don't quite understand him and then they say, "Sorry, I didn't understand what you said." Then he has a chance to say it again. "Stupid is not a good word to say," Teddy says looking at them intently.

The exact wording of the responses varies, but everyone agrees with him – the high school student on her first day of a practicum, the community college student who's visiting, and Madeline's mother when she brings her to school for the afternoon. After she agrees with him, Teddy moves on to another favorite topic.

"Can you say Dumbo?" he asks.

"Dumbo," she says with emphasis and then he is off to sit on the rug and wait for music time to begin.

"I Dropped It"

When I come out of the school to greet the children for the day, Sarah is sitting on the sidewalk in front with her mother standing guard. With her legs set straight out in front of her, Sarah's hands are moving along the rough cement between her legs. She is rocking her head from side to side singing a tune I can't identify.

Her mother warns me that Sarah seems to be searching for tiny things from the ground and rugs at home and often puts them in her mouth. I hadn't seen Sarah do this in the first weeks of working with her, so I ask if this behavior is something new. Assuring her that we will be watchful, I also tell Sarah's mother that this use of her fingers to find small items might be a way Sarah is developing the sensitivity she will need to use Braille. This week the Vision Specialist began labeling things in our room with Braille labels, just to give Sarah exposure. Sarah tolerates our help running her fingers over the labels as we name the chairs, the tables and her worktable. Teddy has discovered the Braille labels and is very interested in them so we explain that someday this is how Sarah will read.

Later at the end of opening circle, we bring Sarah her schedule board to signal the transition to work time. We guide her hand to find the tiny chair held on her schedule board with a square of Velcro. "Music time is all…" we start and pause. "Done," she says and then, feeling the little chair in her hands, her steady little voice continues. "Now it is time for work."

The chair is the symbol we use for work time. Does she understand that it is a chair? Does she think it has anything in common with the chair she will now go to find? Enough right now for her to associate it with work time, to orient to the sound of a voice and to make the eight foot independent journey from her place on the rug to the chair at her work table.

"Stand up," we say. "Find your chair." This directs her away from the music circle.

Lilly waits at the table for her and says quietly, "Come here, Sarah. Find your chair."

Sarah starts to walk forward guided by the sound of Lilly's voice. When her outstretched hand bumps the back of the orange cube chair, Sarah takes hold along the top and moves closer to climb in over the back of the chair.

> *There are so many times I feel ill-prepared to help this child. I have never worked with a blind child before, so I feel that I am learning as we go, giving guidance to the other staff even though I am not sure at times about what we are doing. It reminds me of the early days of this program when I was trying to put into practice things that I had seen in other classes or heard about at a conference. One of the fascinating things about teaching is that we must always be ready for children who challenge what we know. That can be an uncomfortable experience and at times I leave school in the late afternoon feeling inadequate for the challenge of helping to reach Sarah.*

Once Sarah is at the table, we guide her hands to feel for the first shape on her schedule board. "Match," we say and help her match the sandpaper square she has taken off the schedule board to the sandpaper square on her first workbox. The box is full of objects - some familiar and others new today. We've been working with Sarah to help her to learn to identify and name objects in her daily environment.

"What is it?" Lilly says as she puts the tennis ball in Sarah's hands.

"Ball," Sarah responds. "That's right," Lilly affirms and hands her a metal spoon next.

"'Poon," Sarah says. I cue Lilly to up the ante. "Say 'It's a spoon,'" she prompts and Sarah expands her language saying, "It's a 'poon." Then Lilly praises her and gives her a hug and a tickle.

"What is this?" Lilly asks and puts a bristle block in her hand. Sarah passes it from one hand to the other, feeling the small plastic rows. She has been learning to push these together, to stack a growing pile in front of her on the table. But she does not know their name.

"What is it?" Lilly asks again, and then she gives Sarah the name. "It's a bristle block."

Sarah copies with three syllables that come out sounding like "bit-tle bock".

"Ask her again," I cue from behind. When Lilly asks again, Sarah remembers all by herself and says, "It's a bit-tle bock." Lilly and I both clap and Sarah smiles as she drops the bristle block down the side of her chair.

I decide to join this game. "What did you do?" I ask, tickling her gently. "Did you drop it?"

"Pick it up," I say guiding her hand as she leans to one side and searches the floor with her hand until she finds the block. "Pick it up," I say again and she picks it up and holds it out to me.

Next I give her the ball again. She puts it in her lap, names it and then holds it against the side of her cube chair. When she lets it drop there is a tiny thud as the ball hits the floor.

"What did you do?" I say with excitement. "Say, 'I dropped it.'"

Sarah repeats, "I dropped it." On we go, inventing a game that may come back to haunt me. But for now it has completely captured her attention as we try wooden blocks and small metal cars that make different noises when they drop. She is smiling and laughing as she slides each new item down the side of her chair.

Hide the Bus

It's a rainy morning so we must all go more or less straight to the classroom. This is different from the routine we established ten days ago. Since Samuel and Teddy arrive full of energy in the morning, going to the playground for fifteen minutes before music circle proved to be a good way to start the day.

One morning last week, I was walking Sarah toward the playground to meet the other children when I said, "Let's go slide." At that she immediately sat down on the sidewalk and said, "All done slide." Then it dawned on me that Sarah doesn't like the open space of the unfamiliar playground.

Earlier we had initiated a behavior plan to deal with Sarah's sitting down in the hall instead of walking. The plan had many steps. First the teacher should say "Take a break," and then set a timer. When the timer rings, the teacher says "All done break." This behavioral approach made sense in one way but it completely missed the point in another way.

So that morning, when she was in sit down mode on the sidewalk in front of the school, I said, " Let's go play 'Hide the Bus'".

"Hide the bus," she said putting her hand out on the cement and pushing up to stand. We didn't go on toward the playground, but turned instead to go inside the school.

"Yes, we'll play 'Hide the Bus'. Now find the wall," I told her and she reached her right hand out to trail the ceramic tile of the wall while I held the other hand.

"Hide the bus," she said as we started up the ramp toward our wing of the school.

"Yes, find the railing," I cued and when she did I let go of her other hand and she made her way up the ramp and around the corner. On she went, slowly at first but steadily, until we finally arrived at our classroom.

Then we played "Hide the Bus" with one of her favorite toys, a colorful plastic bus with a small yellow switch on one side. When the switch is turned on it activates musical choices. When Sarah presses one raised key the bus announces, "Push a number". Then she feels for the numbers on the side of the bus and presses one for a counting rhyme. If she hits another button a strange little whistle blows a rendition of "*I've Been Working on the Railroad*".

The game is to take the bus and move away from Sarah, across the circle rug, and then say, "Find the bus". You switch it on for just a short rendition of one of these medleys so that Sarah can learn to locate the toy by sound.

"Find the bus," she says as she starts to move across the rug toward the sound. On it goes with Sarah finding the bus, switching it on for a few minutes and then holding the bus out and announcing, "Hide the bus".

It's become a favorite routine for Sarah to play this game with a teacher first thing each morning, while Teddy and Samuel run off some steam on the playground. So this morning when the weather brings us all inside at the same time, the routine is broken. We come into the room together and are going right over to the rug for music circle. In the bustle and noise of helping Samuel and Teddy put their things away in their cubbies, I hear Sarah's voice from over at the rug.

"Hide the bus," she says. "Hide the bus."

We try to move on, to begin our music circle right away. But Sarah becomes more and more upset. We are disrupting her routine. "No music time," she calls out when Lilly gives her the schedule card with the little cardboard guitar that signifies that it's time for singing.

No matter what phrases we try, there is no way to explain to her that because it's a rainy day, our plan is to go right into circle time, skipping over the activity she expects to be first. The more we talk, the more frustrated Sarah becomes and she begins to hit the back of her hand against her mouth in response to all our words.

Finally she calms down enough to try again. "Hide the bus!" she says and I realize then that if we want her to believe in the power of her words, we need to change our plans. So we tell Teddy and Samuel we are going to teach them a new game first and then we will have music time. Given the promise of a game, they are both able to handle this change and are soon excitedly taking turns carrying the bus over to a new spot and calling out to Sarah, "Find the bus."

It ends up being one of those magical moments when something you never planned turns out to be a new breakthrough. Sarah is playing the game with the two boys, responding to their laughter and delight in finding this new way to play with her and the rainy morning is saved.

Playing in the Leaves

Julia stands right in front of Jonah, reaches across to touch his nose and makes a little honking sound. He smiles just a little, hands still in his pockets, standing under the golden tree where we are looking for leaves. Julia pretends to honk his nose again and this time he smiles more widely. Dressed in one of her colorful outfits with patterns all over her dress and different colored stripes on her tights, Julia runs off laughing while Jonah stays standing under the tree. Other children are running around him, picking up leaves and talking about their color or size. But Jonah never moves to pick up a leaf until Lilly comes by and touches him gently on the back.

"Jonah, pick up a leaf," she says quietly and he does. Just one at first but then Julia comes by and gives him one more honk on the nose. This seems to turn on a switch and Jonah begins to run after her, finally joining the other children running through the leaves that cover the ground under the tree.

Later we go out back to the playground that Teddy calls "the last playground" because it is the last one we began to use this year. When we walk around the school and come to the playground, all the children drop their backpacks on the grass and run up the sloping hill to claim a swing or to get in line for the rusty old slide.

Jonah takes his backpack off too, throws it on the grass and comes to stand at the top of the hill at a distance from the foot of the slide. It takes me a little while to notice him because my attention is focused on the line of children taking turns to climb up the slanted metal steps of the old slide.

"Jonah," I call to him, "come and have a turn on the slide." As soon as I ask, he begins to make his way over. Jennifer is just starting up the ladder, challenged by the need to coordinate stepping with alternate feet while pulling up with her arms.

"Jonah wants to come with you," I say to her, knowing that a hint will be all she needs to adopt him for the rest of the afternoon. Every time she comes down, she calls out to him, "Jonah, come on then." And he follows her, over and over, laughing a little when she tries to make room for him to sit next to her on the slide.

Later, when we have gone inside for snack time, Jonah settles into a seat at the table he always chooses but as usual doesn't make any request for food or drink. So far he's still not had any snack at school.

"Would you like a cracker or juice?" I ask him a little later. He's quiet for a few minutes but finally he shakes his head to signify "No".

"You could say, 'No thanks,'" I say and after a pause he does. "No thanks," he offers quietly.

But then he stretches his napkin over his empty cup, looks up at me and asks seriously, "Why can't I just shake my head?"

Now There Are Five

Our morning circle has grown from three children to five and we are working hard to keep up with the new arrivals, Peter and Alex. Alex, a tow-headed boy with bright blue eyes, is a just a visitor at this point, coming to us from the regular integrated preschool next door. He joins us for music time every morning because it seems a good way for us to help figure out what he needs and whether he would be better served by the intensive program in our classroom.

Alex began the school year in the Head Start center in town but they soon became concerned about his very short attention span. He never sat down during their group meeting times and spent the morning in almost constant motion, moving from one activity center to another without engaging in any play with the materials.

Alex's atypical language also concerned the staff at the Head Start center. Whenever they asked him a question, he would just repeat the question back to them. He didn't follow the directions they gave to the group and seemed completely lost much of the time.

One thing we have learned about Alex already is that he cries whenever anyone else cries. Given the fact that Sarah already imitates Samuel when he cries, we've now added a second imitator to this chain. But so far Alex is completely silent with his tears and doesn't add to the general noise level even though he screws up his face and tears run down his cheeks.

Another thing we've learned is that Alex is a darter. I don't know any other way to describe it. He comes in to join our music time and is led over to sit in one of the chairs at our circle. He smiles in response to my greeting him and stays in the chair for only a minute before he jumps up and darts over to another place in the room.

So far we've already tried several different approaches. Often an adult sits behind him and helps to keep him in the chair by applying deep pressure to his shoulders. At other times a teacher crosses her arms over in front of Alex and tries to gently secure him in the chair while we sing one song. A few times we decide to see what will happen if we let him go. Sometimes he just makes a circle and comes right back, but at other times he gets interested in something in another part of the room and is gone for quite a while.

Today I decide to try putting the rice bag on his lap. Covered in soft brown corduroy, the five pound bag of rice helps some children to feel anchored and secure, to stay longer for an activity or a song. At first when I place the heavy bag on his lap, Alex pushes it away with a protest. So I put the bag on my lap and pat it often, smiling each time I do this. Alex watches this for a few minutes and then reaches over for the brown bag. He tolerates my putting it back on his lap and we go on to the next song choice. Teddy has chosen a song that we usually sing standing up but there is no way we are going to do that when Alex has settled for the first time all morning. So we sing the song sitting down, pretending to be pirates by stamping our feet rather than jumping up and down.

Even on the playground, Alex's attention span for most activities is very short. He'll get on a tricycle, ride for a few minutes and then suddenly get off. He'll run over to one of the wagons and climb in while another child is pulling it around the circle painted on the asphalt. All of a sudden Alex will stand up and jump out of the wagon, never asking the other child to stop first. He is in almost constant motion.

So I am amazed today when I begin to play catch with him outside and he stays with the activity longer than I expect.

"Alex, look," I call out the first time and, as soon as he looks toward me, I throw the yellow playground ball to him. He catches it and throws the ball high in the air but back in my direction. "I caught it," I say and then decide I should just stick with the present tense. "Catch," I say every time he catches it. "Throw," I call out just before sending the ball back to him. Alex looks right at me and holds out his hands to catch the ball.

Peter, the other new child, came to our class after it became clear to the teachers at his child care center that there is something very different about the way he is learning. At first his parents were very reluctant to have their child labeled as a child with special needs. For many parents that label carries a stigma that brings back memories of how children with learning problems were treated during their own years in school. They had declined the day care director's recommendation last May to have Peter referred to the public schools for an evaluation.

By the time we meet Peter he has had a neurological evaluation during the summer and received a diagnosis on the autism spectrum. Faced with that diagnosis, his parents decided to contact the public schools and refer their son for services. First of all we are required to do our own assessment, so I go with Eliza, our speech therapist, to observe Peter at his child care center.

We planned for Eliza to get there first and begin working with him on the speech and language evaluation. By the time I come in to observe them, they're sitting on the floor in a large room that the children will use later for climbing toys and tricycles. Now Eliza and

Peter are the only two people in the large room and they are sitting across from each other on a blue mat on the floor. Eliza's taking toys out of a small bag one at a time and holding them out to Peter. She hopes that he will spontaneously name the object and then she'll hand it to him and let him play with it for a few minutes before she pulls out the next object. Peter looks up when I come into the room, his dark brown eyes bright and eager as they play this new game.

"This is Marion," Eliza says. "She's here to play with you too."

Peter smiles in my direction and shifts his slight frame from a kneeling position to sit with his legs crossed as he leans over to see what's in the red plaid bag in front of Eliza.

Eliza pulls out a yellow plastic car and holds it up in front of her, expecting Peter to be interested enough to name it. He doesn't say anything, just reaches his hand out in a silent request to have the toy. When Eliza gives him the little car, he immediately pushes it back and forth in front of him on the mat but doesn't say a word. Out of the ten objects she goes on to present, Peter only names two saying "ba" for the ball and "meow" for the cat.

The striking thing as we continue to test Peter is how happy and cooperative he is but how little language we hear him use. Later he looks carefully at the pictures in the test booklet I spread out on the table in front of him, but he doesn't point to the right picture when I ask him to choose from a group of three or four common objects. He also isn't able to follow verbal directions when we ask him to perform simple tasks during our testing.

When I take Peter back to join his class, I stay to observe him with the other children. The children are moving back and forth in the small room, playing a game that involves loading dishes and pretend food into little carts and wagons. Peter watches what they are doing for a minute and then helps a little girl add more items to her grocery cart before they push it across the room together. He's been in this day care center for over a year and knows the routines well. As I observe him at play, it's clear that he watches the other children carefully and takes his cues from them.

Later when the children gather to sing a few songs and listen to a story, Peter sits next to them in the small circle but I can see that he isn't joining in any of the songs. When the teacher begins to read the story, Peter turns toward the little boy sitting next to him and begins looking over his shoulder at the pictures in another book that child holds in his lap.

By the end of our evaluation, it's clear to us that Peter's very limited expressive language is only part of the problem. He is also struggling to understand what people say to him, trying to figure things out from visual clues. We schedule a meeting with his parents to review the assessments, and all agree that Peter should begin attending our program so he can have the specialized support he needs.

After only two days at school it's clear that Peter could be a poster child for the TEACCH model of structured teaching that is the foundation of our program. Peter takes to the visual schedule right away.

"P for Peter," he says when we show him his name card for the first time yesterday. He lines it up carefully to match the name on his schedule board. Already he's learning to take a card off for the next activity. At work time he's learning to match the shapes on his work schedule to those on the boxes lined up on the shelf next to him.

But Peter is completely stumped by language. "Arms up," I say to him today during an assessment session. He smiles at me and repeats the word "arms" but he does not move his arms.

"Clap," I say next and he looks at me closely but doesn't move.

I try another direction: "Stand up." This time he stands up tentatively and leans on the table. I smile across at him and reach out to touch his shoulder as I say, "Great job. Give me five." He responds either to the words or to the gesture I have used, giving him a visual cue by holding my two hands up. He slaps my hands and yells, "Five." With that momentary success, I decide it is time to move on to another task and come back to the work we will have to do on verbal directions.

I take out two little cups, pretend to drink from one and then hand Peter an identical cup. He immediately pretends to drink from the cup I hand him. When I blow on the little cup I am holding as if to cool it off, Peter imitates that quickly.

Next I take out a little alphabet block and set a plastic clown on top. "Do this," I say, handing him an identical block and clown. He puts his little clown on top of his block facing my clown.

"Hi," he says holding his clown closer to mine. "Hi clown," I say back.

"Hi clown," he repeats and then adds some jargon ending with something that sounds like, "See you."

"See you later," I say as my clown jumps off the block.

"See later," he repeats and jumps his clown down too.

Peter has easily imitated my actions, a skill that is often very difficult for many children on the autism spectrum. When a child isn't able to imitate simple actions the way Peter has, one of the first goals is to painstakingly teach them to do that through repeated one on one teaching. But Peter has shown not only that he can easily imitate but that he can initiate pretend play. When he spontaneously uses his limited language to talk for his small clown and greet mine, Peter has taken the play to a more advanced level. It's a very positive indicator of his potential to expand his social and play skills.

Every morning Teddy asks Peter how old he is. For days Peter doesn't understand the question, so we give him a cue to say "three." Today when Teddy asks him, Peter holds up three fingers and says "three" without any cue from us.

Teddy is very interested in how old everyone is these days and also wants to know how old he was when we did different things.

"How old was I when we went to the fire station," he asks today.

"You were 4," Lilly says. "That was in October."

"And now I'm 4 ½!" he answers.

Then he asks, "How old was I when I had my birthday party at school?"

"You were just four. That was your birthday to turn four."

"And I stuffed my face," he says laughing. That is his joke of the week. Later Teddy draws a picture of a very fat fish and then dictates a story about a fish that stuffed his face. Every time a new adult comes into the classroom he rushes over to have them read his story out loud again.

Peter is like a human sponge waiting to absorb new words every day. When he comes off the van this morning, he is proudly holding the handle of a new rolling backpack. Three days ago when I showed him the picture of a blue backpack, he had no word for it.

"What is it?" I asked. "Blue," he said, pointing to the color of the cloth.

"Backpack," I said. "Backpack," he repeated.

"What is it?" I asked again to see if he could still remember.

"Backpack," he said proudly.

The next two days we repeated the same exercise using photo cards from a language set. Then this morning when he jumps down from the van, he reaches back into the van, takes hold of the green handle and sets his backpack down on the sidewalk in front of us.

"Backpack," he declares and then he turns around to show us the picture on the back of his gray jacket.

"Buzz Lightyear," he says and points to the front of his new backpack. There on the new backpack from his grandfather is the same picture of Buzz Lightyear.

"You have Buzz Lightyear on your backpack too," Lilly says and Peter nods proudly. Then he points toward the sidewalk to the playground. "Where did he go?" he says, using a phrase that doesn't quite say what he means.

"Let's go to the playground," I model.

"Yes, playground!" Peter says and with that he takes hold of the green handle and heads for the playground, dragging Buzz Lightyear along behind him.

Home Visit to Alex

We've known that Alex can read his name but when Lilly and I make a home visit today, we learn that he can read much more than we realized. We ring the doorbell and go down the four steps to their basement apartment. Alex's mother Tara opens the door wide to welcome us in, speaking quietly so she doesn't wake Alex who is sound asleep on the couch behind her.

"He didn't get to sleep 'til really late last night," she says, "and then he got up real early this morning when his Dad was leaving for work. He fell asleep again right after breakfast and I didn't have the heart to wake him up."

In the weeks ahead we will learn that Alex's sleep patterns at night are often erratic and then he sleeps late in the morning and misses coming to school. Now Alex is curled up at one end of the couch, a bright comforter wrapped tightly around his slim figure shows Winnie the Pooh, Eeyore and Tigger marching in a repeated pattern. His light hair is tousled and he has one hand tucked up under his chin. It's the first time we have ever seen Alex so still.

While Alex sleeps peacefully on the couch, we have a chance to talk with Tara about the concerns she's had for some months; about her worry that Alex doesn't talk like other kids.

"But he's really smart," she says. "Wait 'til you see him use the computer."

She settles back onto the couch next to Alex and gently strokes the comforter along the length of his legs. "The trouble is he doesn't pay any attention to what I say. So I can't even take him to the swings and the playground over there," she says, pointing to a grassy area with swings and a sandbox between their apartment building and the next.

"There's no fence and I can't trust him. When he decides to run, he just goes and I can't keep up with him. So I have to keep him inside more than I'd really like to."

I notice Alex beginning to rustle under the cover and then he sits up suddenly and gives us a wide smile. "Oh hi," he says, pushing the comforter onto the floor and climbing over the back of the couch. He goes over to the little yellow table in one corner near the kitchen and picks up a piece of toast that is sitting on the table.

"That's always how he is," his mother says. "He never sits down and eats like you would think a four year old could. He's always moving around. So I put his food on the table and he comes by and gets some when he wants it. My mother-in-law says I shouldn't just let him do that, that I should teach him to sit down and eat his meals at the table. But I don't know - that just doesn't work with Alex."

By now Alex has finished the toast and he goes over and climbs up on a chair to reach the computer that is on a table in one corner of the living room.

"He really loves that computer," Tara tells us. We all watch as Alex works on his own, maneuvering the mouse to open up a game with Disney figures moving across the screen.

"That's his favorite game," Tara says, "and nobody ever really taught him how to do it. We can't figure out how he did it but Jeff and I think he can read…at least some of the words."

Lilly and I move over closer and stand behind Alex to watch as he uses the mouse to choose the printed words that match each picture on the screen. He suddenly switches to another game and we watch him choose the printed words that answer simple questions.

"It's the only time he ever sits still," Tara comments. "It doesn't make any sense to me. How can a little kid read when he doesn't even know how to talk yet?"

Her question is a good one and we leave promising to do all we can to figure out what is going on with Alex's learning.

"I'm glad he's finally got somewhere to go where they can help him," Tara says, running her fingers through Alex's tousled hair as he keeps his focus on the computer screen. "You gotta keep a really close eye on him. He's really fast and he can just take off on you."

"We've seen that already," Lilly says "and we'll be sure to keep close to him."

"Well I guess it will be alright then," Tara says as I kneel down to tell Alex good-bye before we leave.

The Parent Conference

Jonah sits cross legged on the rug each day, one of the first children to find a place around the oval rug for the music circle that begins each afternoon class. He always chooses an alphabet letter somewhere between Q and U, but is not rigid about which one he needs to sit on.

We begin with a sign language routine using our hands to make the signs for "Good afternoon, I'm happy to see you." Then we do it again adding voices to the signs. All of the other children join in some way, hands moving more or less in unison. But Jonah sits with his hands in his lap or tucked firmly under his legs and never signs or speaks a word.

When it's his turn to be the "guitar helper," he will unlock the case and hand me the guitar. On a day when it's his turn to choose a song, he will stand up and select a picture card from the choices. Then he'll Velcro it onto the purple cardboard on the easel and announce the name of the song to the other children. But he never sings. All through September and most of October, he sits and watches the other children but does not sing or sign along with any of the songs.

When I meet with his mother today for a parent conference, I'm amazed at her answer when I ask what Jonah likes to do at home when he's free to play whatever he wants.

"All he does right now is sing," she says. "He gets out his father's guitar and he tells us all that we have to sit down in a circle on the living room rug. He must be imitating you because there are definite routines to what he says. I think he knows every song you've ever sung, all the words. And we have to sit and listen."

This is a complete surprise to me and it changes my sense of what he is doing there every day. All we see are fleeting smiles and his wide blue eyes moving from my direction to watch other children as they sing. Silent and without any other sign of what he is doing, Jonah is memorizing them all, one song after another with all the verses and actions.

"It's all he wants to do right now," his mother says. "He goes through one song after another, holding his father's guitar and strumming at random. It's really the way he learns. Last time it was dribbling a ball – he'd never done it and then that was all he wanted to do over and over again for two weeks."

"Mommies Are Not at School"

Samuel has thrown all the dolls out of the low wooden cradle and he is climbing in, bare feet first. Settling down into the cradle, he spreads the little flannel blanket over his body and tucks it up to his chin. His pale feet stick out from the end of the blanket.

"I can still see your toes," Teddy says. "I don't like to see toes." So Teddy takes another little blanket off one of the dolls thrown on the floor and spreads it over Samuel's bare feet.

"That's better," he says as he lays his head down in Samuel's lap. It's an awkward gesture and clearly does not suit Samuel's idea.

"No, no," he says, "Get here." He slides over to one side of the little cradle, creating a thin space that he seems to think can accommodate the much sturdier Teddy.

But Teddy decides to move over to pile pretend fruit and vegetables into the play sink instead and Samuel settles back down into the cradle sucking his thumb.

Later in the afternoon it is time to take the class to the library for our weekly story hour with Mrs. Russell. Soon after she starts reading the story to the group of children, Samuel calls out suddenly, "The library is closed."

Mrs. Russell turns to him and says quietly, "No, Samuel – the library is open." Then she goes on reading the story. A few minutes later he calls out again, "The library is closed." But this time he is pointing to the Venetian blinds that are closed to block the view to the back play area.

"Oh, the blinds are closed," she says and with that she opens them a little before returning to the story. Less than a page later, Samuel calls out again, "The library is closed." This time before she pauses I quietly say, "Probably time to just ignore him – he's stuck."

So she goes on reading and soon Samuel settles down on the rug and listens to the last part of the story book.

When we come back from the library, it's time for the children to go to their small group activities. Teddy is working at the blue table with his small group, stuffing fiberfill into a tube sock to make a tall, lean snowman. It's not quite the round, plump effect I was hoping for. Meanwhile Samuel is an escapee from another table where his small group is playing a lotto game. The pace soon became too slow for him and he is up and away roaming the room.

"I'm going to whip his butt," Samuel is yelling as he tries to get close enough to Teddy to give him a hit. I have no idea how this one started; Teddy may have said something to Samuel about needing to go back to his table. Teddy is bothered by anyone breaking the rules – real or imagined. Whatever started it, Samuel now has only one thing on his mind.

"I'm going to whip his butt," he says again as he runs around to the other side of the table. By now Lilly has taken up a position nearby to shield Teddy but Samuel keeps looking for a way in, circling the room and coming back.

Finally I take him firmly by one hand and say, "Come on Samuel, we're going to take a walk." With that we are out the classroom door and headed down the hall before he can protest. As soon as we are out of the room, Samuel calms down.

"That's James' kindergarten," he says as we walk by the next classroom and just then our former student and his friend from the daily van ride comes out the kindergarten door.

"Hello James," Samuel says. "I'm happy to see you."

He uses the line we repeat every day at the opening of circle. Now all these weeks later, the phrase is completely appropriate for greeting James in the hallway and the two boys give each other a hug.

"James is not in my class," Samuel says as we walk on down the hall.

"You're right, but James rides the van with you and later you can ride home to see your Mommy."

"Mommy is not at school," Samuel says repeating a line he uses whenever we say anything about his mother. His mother tells us that anytime she says anything about one of his teachers at home Samuel responds, "Miss Lilly or Miss Maria or Miss Marion is not here."

Zachary, a slim sandy haired boy in the afternoon class, has been crying in protest every day lately when his mother drops him off at school. "I want my Mommy to stay," he says tearfully.

"Mommies are not at school," Samuel says emphatically. "Mommy is at home!"

"I want my Mommy to stay at school," Zachary says again. By now Teddy has come over to see what is going on.

"Are you sad when your Mommy goes?" Teddy asks Zachary who nods in response, tears still running down his cheeks.

"I was sad when my grandmommy and papa left," said Teddy. "But now my Mommy and Daddy are babysitting me."

Earlier this fall his parents went away for a few days while his grandparents came to stay from California.

"When your parents are home we call it 'taking care of me' – not babysitting," I say to Teddy.

"Well, I like to call it 'babysitting me,'" he says, "so that is what I say."

The Power of the Match

It is an amazing thing, given our expanding cast of characters, to see the power of our model based on the structured teaching approach used by the TEACCH program at the University of North Carolina. Their work is rooted in the philosophy that there is a "culture of autism" and that many individuals with autism share certain learning characteristics. The TEACCH model is designed to provide an educational approach that is sensitive to this culture of autism. As I see Peter and Alex latch on to the structure the program provides, I am convinced again of the powerful match between this program model and the learning style of many children with autism spectrum disorder (ASD).

Because the TEACCH model uses visual strategies, children like Peter and Alex are able to use their visual strengths to begin to understand what is expected of them. When we first presented Peter with a work schedule strip with four different shapes in a row, he immediately named each shape. Then we showed him how to take the first workbox and match the first shape from his work schedule to the identical shape on the front of the box. It is a visual way of showing him what his work for the day will be.

"Match," we said, helping him to pull the first shape from the strip and attach it to the Velcro on the matching shape on the first box. Within two days he and Alex both learned to use this visual system to select the workboxes from the row on a shelf to their left. One of the boxes for Peter usually included a sheet of paper with one step commands set up on a data grid.

"Touch your nose," I said to Peter when he first began and he would look at me with a puzzled expression on his face.

He had no idea what I was asking him to do and I was not offering any gestures or picture cues to help him out. So we began to work on building his understanding by practicing a set of simple commands. We would give him a command, pause and then model it so that he could learn to match actions to words. Then we would fade our prompts as he began to do the tasks on his own.

"Touch nose," we can say now and when he does this independently we make a small + next to that command on the grid. Then we move on to repeat this process for six to eight commands on his list.

Yesterday Peter was drawing pictures as a final activity during his work session. Earlier we had been taking data as I ran through an expressive language practice session, presenting photos for him to name verbs and common objects. Now he was doing free drawing, a favorite activity.

"You eyes," he said to me after he had finished drawing a picture of himself and Sponge Bob. I assumed he was now going to draw a picture of me.

"Here are my eyes," I said, pointing to them.

"Good job," Peter said and made a perfect + on the paper in front of him.

"Touch nose," he said next and when I did he made another + on his paper.

I was amazed. In six years of using this model we have had several children who love to turn the tables, present the pictures and ask the questions. But Peter was not only giving the directions, he was taking the data. He had taken the whole procedure in, learning far more than we had realized.

Alex continues to be mystified by questions and verbal directions without any picture clues. His strategy for dealing with auditory input is to repeat exactly what he hears you say.

"What's your name?" he repeated until we showed him the name card. He cannot touch body parts on command or follow a direction. He doesn't answer any questions unless there is a visual prompt.

Today we are working with shaped pictures of vehicles with magnetic backing. I hold one up in front of my eyes to encourage him to look at me.

"Look Alex. What is it?"

Interested in the colorful pictures, he looks at me in spite of his general reluctance to make eye contact.

"It's a fire," he answers for the fire engine.

"It's a fly," he calls out for the airplane.

Then he goes on to name a bicycle, a police car and a ship.

"A ship goes in the …," I say, hoping he can fill in the blank. No answer.

"An airplane flies in the …," I try next. Alex just looks at me with one of his sudden smiles but gives no response to the question.

Ladies and Gentlemen

Small steps climb up to the top of the curving slide on the wooden structure in front of the school. Alex goes up the steps, runs to the top of the slide and watches as Teddy and Samuel come past him and disappear down the slide.

Alex runs back down the steps to where I am standing and in his high little voice says, "Oh, hi Marion". Then he turns, climbs back up the stairs to the top of the slide and hesitates a moment before running back down and starting the routine all over again.

After watching him repeat this sequence for the second day in a row, I climb up the stairs behind him to the top of the slide. "Let's slide down," I say as I sit myself down at the top of the curving slide. I pat my lap and say "Sit down."

"Sit down," Alex repeats as he plops himself down in my lap. I put my arms around him so he won't have his arms out where they could be hurt as we go around the curves.

"Ready – set – go" I say and we are off down the slide. I can't see his face until we're at the bottom and then I see that Alex is smiling. I now have a new understanding of why Teddy calls this the bumpy slide because the ridges in the metal hit at regular intervals.

Alex starts back up the steps, goes half way and then turns around to come back down to where I am standing. Curious to see if he'll ask to do it again, I wait.

"Oh, hi Marion," he says with a smile as he takes my hand.

"Say 'I want slide,'" I cue him.

"Want slide," he repeats and with that we head back up the steps together.

"Sit down" I say as I sit down and this time before I need to pat my lap, he is sitting in it.

"Slide," I say, "Ready – set …."

"Go" Alex calls out and we are off again, bumping over the metal ridges as we speed down the slide.

Later at work time I show him a picture of a child going down a slide.

"What is he doing?" I ask Alex, holding the picture up for him to look at it.

"I want slide," he says.

"He is sliding," I say and he repeats the verb. Next I show him a picture of a child crawling. "What is he doing?" I ask. He doesn't say anything but drops from his chair to the floor, crawls under the table to my side and then turns around and crawls back to his chair.

"That's right - crawling. The boy is crawling."

Alex looks at the pictures again and repeats one word, "crawling."

The next picture shows a little girl standing with one hand on a colorful microphone that is on a stand in front of her. It is supposed to elicit the response that the girl is singing.

"What is she doing?" I ask Alex.

He looks intently at the picture for a few minutes without responding so I repeat the question, "What is she doing?"

Alex suddenly stands up and says in a louder voice than usual, "Ladies and gentlemen, boys and girls."

It is a window into the fascinating learning style of this child. It reminds me of a moment with another child years ago, early in my teacher training. She had great difficulty remembering the names of objects but she could read many words. We were using toy fruit and vegetables from a language kit, trying to help her learn the names of common foods.

I handed her the plastic orange and asked her, "Judy, what is it?" She turned it over in her hand and, looking at the stamp on the bottom, said, "It's a made in Japan."

Alex's learning is more complex. He does not know many verbs yet but he names many common objects. Verbs are more abstract because by definition they involve action and therefore keep changing. He seems to learn by associating chunks of language with scenes in videos or with experiences he remembers.

Somewhere in a video, he must have seen someone stand at a microphone and say those words, probably in a scene with a ringmaster at a circus. Alex doesn't label the microphone and he can't name the action singing or talking. But somewhere in his memory bank he pairs the words of a ringmaster with the picture I have just shown him and that triggers his surprise announcement.

Making Transitions

Transitions are difficult for children who reside anywhere on the autism spectrum, and therefore they are often challenging for the adults who shepherd them through a day. Some days the transitions in our classroom consume more time, energy and ingenuity than anyone could imagine who had not spent a day with us.

The first transition of the day begins when the children arrive on the vans or with their parents and we head to the playground, weather permitting. This trip to the playground is usually easy for everyone except Sarah. But leaving the playground to go inside is a major problem for Alex. After three days of needing to pick him up and carry him into school, we work together to come up with a better plan. We decide to use his reading skills to help us through the transitions he is resisting.

I make cards for each routine event, using a large font on the computer and then add a relevant picture symbol from his schedule cards. We laminate the cards, punch holes in the top and put them on a ring. The first day we are ready to try the cards, I meet Alex at the bus with the ring of pictures attached to a cord around my neck with the cards turned over so only the blank side shows.

Later when it is time to go in from the playground, we give all the children the usual warning. "Five more minutes," Samuel calls out echoing what we had said.

Alex runs wildly over to the playhouse, settles into the tippy red chair for a minute and then runs out the backdoor toward me.

"Oh hi, Marion," he says and I see my opening.

"Look Alex," I say as I turn the card around and bend down so he can see it. The printed words catch his attention at once and he begins to read.

"Playground is all done. Now it is time to go in for music time. Take my hand and we will walk in together."

I would like to say that he smiled, reached up and took the hand that I held out to him and that we walked in together. Of course that didn't happen because the card wasn't magic - not fast magic anyway.

But after days of using the same cards, we begin to see progress. There are times now when he does take the adult's hand and we walk along together, and those times are more and more frequent.

The last card of the day says, "Playground is all done. Now it is time to find Mike's bus. Take my hand and walk with me."

At times he doesn't want playground time to be over, so he won't read beyond the first word of the card. "Playground," he reads with a laugh and then he reads it again, "Playground…..yes, playground," he will say and wait.

But the drive to read always gets the best of him and he reads on, "Playground is all done." And day by day it is getting easier – I have to believe that is true.

During lunch time, Alex has been falling out of his chair and crawling under the table or running across the room disrupting lunch for the other children. After several days of Alex frustrating all the efforts of the rotating cast of staff members who share lunch coverage, we accidentally hit upon a solution to the problem with the transition to lunch time.

When I observed this behavior begin again, I took Alex's hand, led him out to the hall and sat him in one of the cube chairs we use at morning circle. I didn't really have a plan; I just had my own sense of frustration that what we were doing was not working. But I discovered that when I sat him in that cube chair, Alex stayed there. He even stayed there long enough for me to go in and bring his lunch out to the hall. I turned another cube chair over to make it into a small table and set that in front of him, pushing it in so close I essentially boxed him into the chair. I set his macaroni in a bowl on the table in front of him with his favorite green plastic spoon from home. I took a third cube chair and sat on top of that, pushing right up against the little table.

"Oh hi Marion," he said and proceeded to eat his lunch. So that is how we set up his personal lunch table everyday now. We don't set it up out in the hall but place it behind a counter that separates him enough from the other children that he can settle in and eat his lunch. Trapped in one sense, secure in another, he makes his way through the contents of his lunch box, often looking at the pictures with the teacher while he eats.

Teaching "Come Here"

We began teaching Alex to respond to the direction "Come here" as a safety precaution. One day he had gone to the top of the little hill next to the asphalt area where the children ride bikes in back of the school. When I went toward him to bring him back to the play area, he smiled at me and then took off in the opposite direction around the school building.

Luckily I have long legs and was able to catch up with him, but we knew that once he'd done this, it was likely to become a habit. So we began to teach him to come when we called him. We began one morning when we were on the bike playground and he had just gone a short distance from me up the grassy hill.

"Alex – come here!" I called, crouching down a little holding my arms out wide and wiggling my fingers as I smiled at him. Luckily he came running and I caught him up with a big hug. Then he turned and ran back to the place where he'd started. He was hooked – and proceeded to run down to me again and again when I called his name.

Sometimes I'd swing him around, sometimes I'd tickle him and other times I'd just laugh and give him a big hug. I would never ask him to do anything else. It was all about his just responding to the direction "Come here."

By the next day, when I was far enough away from him that he might not hear the direction, I tried using body language only after I called his name. "Alex," I'd call and then throw my arms wide and wiggle my fingers as I bent down. He would stop where he was, look back at me and come running. It was a new game and he loved it.

By now it is a solid skill and we have been able to use it when we need a quick way to move him off the playground or bring him back when he is primed to run the opposite way down the hall.

Yesterday when Peter saw Alex heading away from the bike play area, he called out to him. "Alex – come here." Then Peter threw out his arms, wiggling his fingers in his bright yellow Sponge Bob gloves. Alex turned, paused just a moment and then ran straight to Peter who gave him a big hug.

Mommy's Birthday Soon

"Mommy's birthday soon," Peter announces as he steps off the van this morning. A little later his mother arrives in the classroom just after we come in from a few minutes on the playground. I tell her what he said when he came off the van and she explains that he has been looking forward to her birthday for days. When he would start talking about her birthday, they would tell him that Mommy's birthday is soon. So he learned the whole phrase and today, on her real birthday, he still calls it "Mommy's birthday soon". She has taken time off on her birthday to come and visit our class for the first time.

When we settle in for music circle, I ask Sarah to tell me her name but she's not ready yet. So I move on to Peter and he eagerly responds, "I Peter", then he turns to flash a smile and a thumbs up sign to his mother who is sitting behind him in a rocking chair. We move on to Alex who is sitting next to Peter.

"What's your name?" I ask Alex. "What's your name?" he repeats with a smile.

I try again to ask him his name. "What's your name?" he repeats again.

Then I ask Lilly to bring me his name card from his picture schedule. When Lilly comes back with the card with his name printed in capital letters, I ask the question once more but this time I hold his name card up in front of him as I finish the question. He points to the card immediately and reads his name, "ALEX".

"Yes, your name is Alex," I say excitedly and Samuel and Teddy both begin to clap because he finally said his own name. Alex breaks into a broad smile as he joins in the clapping and calls out, "Congratulations."

"Congratulations," Samuel calls back at Alex, delighted with this new word that now finds its way into the odd call and response of our morning music time.

Alex is a fascinating fellow – definitely our biggest challenge of this year. He is so mystified by spoken language and yet he can read almost anything we put in front of him. At times we are able to use his ability to read to our advantage.

"Sit down and eat" the little sign says on the lunch table where he now sits with the other children.

"Pull pants down," the first picture card says on the strip posted to the right of the toilet. "Pull your pants down," he read yesterday. But he immediately moved back from the toilet and read the last card, "Pull your pants up," skipping all the steps in between.

Today when he read the first card and said, "Pull your pants down," I showed him the new card I made yesterday with a picture of an M&M candy on it. This captured his interest and Alex unzipped his jeans and pulled them down quickly and then did the same with his Spiderman boxers. I guided him closer to the toilet and as soon as he was there he read the next card, "Stand facing the toilet."

I held a bright red M & M candy out in front of him, rewarding his following the first cards. Alex took it at once, popped it in his mouth and said, "Yes, yes…this is truly delicious." This has to be a line from one of his many videos or books that he has committed to memory.

After three weeks of what we like to think is toilet training, this is as far as we've gotten. The expression "You can lead a horse to water" applies here. You can train a child to stand facing a toilet but so far that is all. He does not go to the bathroom in public places – that is his rule. He only uses the toilet at home.

There are other ways for us to work on this. We probably need to write a social story about using the toilet at home and at school. But of course that takes time and there are not enough hours in the day to make all the visual cue cards, the social stories, the individual language activities I think of as a day goes by.

It is clear that print is a useful and powerful tool for Alex and he can use his reading skill with surprising creativity at times. The other day Stacey, the Occupational Therapist, came into the classroom to get Sarah and take her for a therapy session in her room down the hall. Alex loves to go to the O.T. room with the ball pit, the big balls, bikes and ramps but it was not his turn to go that day.

While Stacey was still in the room helping to move Sarah along, I saw Alex go over to open the clear pink case where we keep all of his schedule cards that we line up left to right on his schedule board to show the plan for the day. He rummaged through his box and then ran across the room. At this point another child claimed my attention. The next time I looked, Alex had dumped Teddy's case of schedule cards on the floor. I thought it was just erratic behavior like when he takes a wooden puzzle from the rack and lifts it up fast so all the pieces go flying through the air and clatter to the floor.

But a minute later I saw that Alex had claimed an O.T. card from Teddy's box and was putting it up on his schedule board. Then he took it off the board, brought it over to Stacey and said, "O.T."

His behavior had not been random at all – it was completely purposeful. He wanted to go to the O.T. room and he knew that when the teacher has put the card on your board, it is your turn. So he had literally taken matters into his own hands! I was so impressed with the planning and problem solving involved in this action that I asked Stacey to take him along too.

This seemed like a good idea at the time but of course today Alex added the O.T. card to his schedule board again. All of my verbal explanations fell short of his understanding.

"No O.T. today." "Not your turn." "No Stacey today."

All my words tangled somewhere in the language center of his brain. After all, the card had worked the other day so why didn't it work today?

"Don't Say Hi"

It's the first morning back after the December vacation and Teddy's returning from a holiday vacation. I see him coming down the hall with his mother, his right arm held out in front of him, waving his hand back and forth as he gets closer.

"Don't say hi to me!" Teddy calls in a loud voice. "Don't say hi!"

"He's a bit on overload from the days with our extended family," his mother says quietly as we meet. "There's a note in his book."

Given that cue, I low key my enthusiasm at seeing him again and walk beside him into the classroom. He announces his prohibition on saying hi to Maria so she catches herself and doesn't greet him the way she would like to. But a few minutes later Sarah arrives with Lilly who has not heard any of this. In her bubbly fashion, Lilly hurries over to Teddy, gives him a quick hug and says, "Hi Teddy, I am so glad to …."

That is as far as she gets because Teddy declares loudly, "Don't say 'Hi Teddy.' " This declaration immediately catches Sarah's attention. Loud noises surprise and distress her and she responds by latching on to a phrase and repeating it over and over. Unfortunately she chooses only the last three words of what Teddy said so she begins repeating: "Say hi Teddy, say hi Teddy". Sarah says it over and over again as she stands just inside the door, unzips her jacket and lets it fall to the floor.

By now Teddy is red in the face as he rushes over to stand next to Sarah. Leaning down to put his face close to the smaller child's, Teddy repeats his request, "Don't say 'Hi Teddy.'"

This elicits another round of "Say hi Teddy, Say hi Teddy" from Sarah.

There is no talking to either of them at this point so I use my size advantage to help Teddy move across the room to sit with me on the rocking chair. Once he has calmed down enough to listen, I try to explain what has just happened.

"Sarah doesn't understand what you want," I say. "She was surprised by your loud voice and when she is scared by a sound she sometimes gets stuck like a tape or a CD. She keeps saying the same words over and over because she is upset."

"But I used my words," Teddy says, his bottom lip quivering and his cheeks still bright red.

"Yes, you did and look, it is alright now. Sarah isn't saying those words. She's not stuck anymore." With that a tentative calm is restored and we can get on with the morning music circle. We do not even consider singing the hello song today. That seems dangerously close to saying hi to Teddy.

A Budding Friendship

It is becoming clearer to us every day that Samuel doesn't really match the profile for most children who earn the diagnosis of autism. When we met him last spring, he had very little language. But he keeps surprising us with how much language he learned over the summer. We planned on using the same structured teaching techniques we used with Teddy when he first came and that we use with Peter now. But Samuel comes to the table already knowing the names of many of the objects and pictures we present during teaching sessions.

He's using short sentences to comment on things that happen in class and to tell us what he did at home with his mother. His language is blossoming in a way that is much more like a typical child than it is like a child with autism.

"Spiderman climbs up the wall," he told me yesterday when he was playing on the climber, going up the ladder with one hand held out in front of him as if he were casting out a web.

When Teddy began to laugh at one of his own jokes about a "tomato hotel" at lunch time today, Samuel looked at him with a frown and said, "That is not funny."

Language is not proving to be a serious problem for Samuel after all. But managing his responses to frustration is proving to be a daily challenge. He can go from calm to intensely angry in the time it takes his block tower to fall off the table after Teddy accidentally bumps against it. That is when Samuel's language fails him. He is so angry that he can't even find the words to say something to Teddy. He falls to the floor, crying in protest.

"I didn't mean to do it, it was an accident," Teddy says, his lower lip trembling as his face begins to redden. "It was just an accident, Samuel," he says bending down to where Samuel is now half under the table.

"Do you want Teddy to help you fix it, Samuel?" Lilly asks him. At first Samuel can't even respond; usually he is too upset by the real or perceived insult when something like this happens that he leaves the scene of the frustration. But as Lilly rubs his back, he begins to calm down enough to find some words.

"You broke my building, Teddy. It is all falled down."

"Are you mad at me Samuel?" Teddy asks, now more curious than upset.

"Yes, I am really mad at you," Samuel says, sitting up and making one of his fiercest faces.

"Well, that's alright because I will help you pick these up and then you don't have to be so mad anymore," Teddy says, watching Samuel's face relax a little as he begins to put the blocks back up on the table.

In spite of his difficulty handling frustration and surprises, Samuel is very interested in playing with other children and this strong interest in socializing is also counter to common behavior for children on the autism spectrum. His first friendship is with Peter and we begin to notice that they often choose to play in the same area of the room during the free play time that follows morning work time and snack. They both love to draw and are exceptionally good at making simple human figures that tell a story. One of Peter's specialties is drawing Sponge Bob Square Pants in a way that is strikingly like the cartoon character. Samuel is more inclined to draw versions of Spiderman that become more complex and detailed each week.

Yesterday Peter brought a crooked little pad of paper that he had made at home by stapling some small pieces of paper together. At first we didn't understand what he was saying when he tried to tell us about it. Finally Lilly figured out that he was calling it "Joe's book" after the notebook that Joe uses on the T.V. program called *Blue's Clues*. On that show, Joe, the host, uses the notebook to draw the clues that will help solve the story puzzle. This may have captured Peter's attention because he often depends on visual clues to help him understand the mystery of language.

Yesterday afternoon we made more small notebooks with covers of bright construction paper and Peter shared them with other children. There are only two notebooks left on the counter when Peter comes over to the art area to draw this morning. Samuel comes over too, following Peter to see what he is doing, and he quickly chooses the red notebook and sits down to begin drawing. That leaves Peter the purple notebook with yellow spots of paint that were splattered on the front yesterday when children were painting pictures of yellow forsythia branches.

At once Peter is frustrated by the yellow spots of paint on the purple cover of the little notebook. I try to turn the notebook over with the back cover on top because that doesn't have any yellow spots of paint. But Peter notices that this means the back of the staples along the top show and before the front of the staples always showed. This small detail means that this notebook is not the same and things that look different or changes in routine do not rest well with Peter.

Earlier this morning Peter forgot to move his name card from his cubby to the top of his picture schedule before he came over to circle. Later when it was time for me to get the name cards from their schedule boards and hold them up one at a time to help children transition from music to work time, I went over myself to get Peter's card from his cubby and bring it over to the circle. I thought it was the quickest way to move us along. Not so! The change in routine caused Peter to immediately break down in tears of frustration.

At times like this we realize how limited his communication skills still are. He's made great headway naming pictures and answering the question "What's she doing?" for 75% of the verb cards in List 1 and List 2. But when something goes wrong, he has very few strategies for "repairing communication". Words literally fail him and he has nowhere to go with his frustration but to dissolve in tears.

Indeed his tears were quite effective in communicating distress and stopping me in my tracks. I put the card back on the Velcro tab at his cubby and came back to where the five boys waited – more or less – on the rug.

"Peter, do you want to go get your name?" I asked and off he went. The fascinating thing to me was that he didn't just go and get the card and bring it to circle.

First he took the card from his cubby and went over to match it to the name printed in the left hand corner of his schedule board. He attached it there, paused a moment and then took it off again and brought it over to the rug. Only then could I hold his name up and ask, "Whose name is this?" "I Peter," he said, calm and secure again.

From a functional point of view, there was absolutely no reason to put Peter's name card on the schedule board first. We had already moved on. But that step had been omitted, and he needed to have things done in the proper order. Peter could not skip a step but he didn't know how to tell us that in words, only through his tears and actions.

Sarah's Story

We should know by now to never say "Okay" after Sarah says "no" and shakes her head to refuse something. At least she appears to be refusing something but it isn't always clear if that is what she really means and that adds to the problem. This is where *our* self-control becomes the issue.

In nine cases out of ten when we respond "okay" without thinking, she will repeat that word over and over again. "Okay, okay, okay," she says as her voice rises with mounting agitation that makes it clear it is really not okay at all. We can safely assume she is very mad or frustrated with our failure to understand whatever it is she is trying to communicate.

Today we are "leaving her be" for a little while after snack time is over. It is my suggestion that Lilly walk over to the rug area with Sarah and then say, "Time to play." We are constantly giving her guidance and I want to see what she'll do if we back off and let her take the initiative.

Lilly sits across from her as she settles into one of the little cube chairs. Since Lilly is silent, Sarah can't really be sure she is still there. Sarah sits quietly for a little while and then begins to sing a fragment of a song I can't recognize. Soon she stands up and walks a few steps until her hands touch the chalk tray along the front wall. She follows the chalk tray until her right hand touches the top shelf in the corner by the windows.

"P-I-A-N-O," she says in a voice similar to that of her spelling toy at home. "P I A N O spells piano."

As she walks a few more steps along the shelf, I hear her voice as she very quietly says, "What do you want to do? Play the piano."

By now she's touching the cloth that covers the shelf where we store the keyboard when it is not in use.

"Sarah, do you want to play the piano?" Lilly asks.

"Yes I do, "she answers.

So Lilly goes over, takes the keyboard out and sets it across two cube chairs where Sarah can reach it. She sets another small chair in front of the keyboard. Sarah feels the back of the chair with one hand and reaches toward the keyboard with the other. In a moment she settles in the chair, tries a few notes to locate her fingers on the keyboard and begins to play "When the Saints Go Marching In." She's found what she wants to do and we've had a clear reminder that we need to give Sarah more space sometimes and let her make choices on her own.

Samuel and Peter have settled into play with the marble maze tower. Sarah finishes playing the piano and is about four feet away from them at the other end of the oval rug. She hears the notes the xylophone plays when the first marble rolls across that part of the maze. She begins to walk sideways across the rug, one arm reaching out to find the source of the sound.

The marble maze is a wonderful wooden construction that stands about four feet high. Soon Sarah locates one side and begins to feel along the wooden trough until a marble launched by another child hits her fingers. She holds the marble for a minute and then puts it back into the trough. She puts her hands up to her ears, anticipating the sound of the marble cascading down the xylophone.

Sarah spends the next twenty minutes exploring the marble maze. "Let her find it," I remind Lilly when she starts to guide Sarah's hand to where the track for the marbles begins at the top.

"Let her find it," Lilly reminds Peter when he starts to take her hand and put it on the marble where it has landed in a little bowl at the bottom of the maze. "Tell her it's at the bottom or on the floor."

Peter gives her this clue and after a few minutes Sarah feels along the track for the marbles, moving her hand down until she is at the base. Her left hand bumps the little wheel at the bottom and she reaches down and finds the marble in the small plastic dish.

"You did it," Peter says and then turning to where I am watching announces, "Look - her did it!"

When Sarah is leaving school in the afternoon, I realize that the trick for us is to figure out what we can say to her that will make sense when she repeats it. *Functional* is the word that Eliza, the speech therapist, always uses to help us focus on what our language goal is for each child. To say "P-I-A-N-O spells piano" is not functional language; it's a memorized fragment.

When I say "Good-bye Sarah" as she walks by me at the end of the day, she repeats it back to me – "Good-bye Sarah." That is not functional. But if I remember to say enthusiastically "Good-bye, see you tomorrow," her repetitive phrase will sound more appropriate. "Good-bye," Sarah responds. "See you tomorrow."

So how many phrases can we think of that work equally well when she repeats them verbatim? Does that really mean they are functional?

A Surprising Development

In spite of all the time and effort we have spent on the toilet training plan, Alex has not gone to the toilet at school. His mother reports that he still won't go to the toilet anywhere except at home.

Ever since he settled into our class in October, we have been working toward the goal of having him use the toilet at school. We've had the picture strip with all the sequential steps hanging on the wall in each toilet stall. He will read them all in sequence but he won't follow the steps. Sometimes if you say, "Okay now, pull down your pants," right after he reads that card, Alex will crouch down in a defensive posture and skip ahead to read the last card.

"Pull up your pants," he reads and then stands up and leaves the bathroom.

So we developed a social story for him. "Alex goes to the bathroom at home" it begins. Then it goes on with three pages about how it is okay to go to the toilet at school. "Okay," he would add every time after reading that line in the story. He was very dramatic as he read and acted out many of the lines.

Alex read the story for the first time one day during 1:1 teaching time. When he finished the book he turned back to the first page, and began to read it again. He read it all the way through two more times before snack time. One line in the book said that when Alex goes to the bathroom at school Ms. Lilly will say, "Hooray for Alex." Each time he read this line Alex would throw his arms up in the air and shout "Hooray".

Later we thought it would be a good idea to have him read the story in the bathroom. So he did. He read it over and over again, day after day in our bathroom and in the quiet bathroom near the speech therapy room.

At regular intervals we tried to coach him to really pull down his pants, to earn an M & M for trying and the triple prize of three candies for going to the toilet. All of this was explained in the book and although he read each paragraph with enthusiasm, he didn't take the bait.

Sometimes he would be calm in his refusal to act and other times he would be more adamant. He kept on reading the book at school until days turned into weeks. We made him an identical book for home and he read it there several times every day.

A week ago his mother wrote a surprising news flash in his home/school notebook. She told us that they had taken Alex to the hospital for an appointment the day before. On the way to the appointment, he went into every bathroom they passed in the halls. Later, on their way out of the building, Alex went into one single bathroom, took off all of his clothes and went pee. His mother was thrilled. It was the first time he had ever used a public toilet.

The next Monday his notebook relayed the news that he had gone to the toilet at a discount store over the weekend. So when he began to read the toilet book on Monday, I just took him by one hand and said, "Let's go see the quiet bathroom." Off we went without a protest to the small bathroom near the speech therapy room. Alex read page two once we were there and then set the book down on the floor.

"Pull down your pants," he read from the strip of pictures posted on the wall and then proceeded to follow the direction. Alex moved closer to the toilet and read, "Stand facing the toilet." After just a minute he sent a steady stream right into the center of the toilet.

"Hooray for Alex," I called out in amazement.

"Hooray for Alex," he said back and then went on with the sequence of cards. "Pull up your pants."

I was caught off guard and all the M & Ms were back in the bathroom by our class but he didn't seem to mind the delay. Once we were back in our class I had him tell the other teachers what had happened. "Hooray for Alex," each one said. "You did it." Then he was off to play with the colored rice in the water table.

The next day soon after he came to school, Alex went right in without any prompting and used the toilet. In the afternoon he went into the bathroom again completely on his own. The first we knew about it was when a teacher from the class next door told us that he hadn't washed his hands after using the toilet. When I went in to coach him to wash he was already in the other toilet stall.

"Pull down your pants," he read. "Stand facing the toilet."

He managed to go pee again – once for each toilet. "Hooray for Alex," he declared and then went to wash his hands.

Later during activity time I noticed him heading into the bathroom again. This time he pointed down into the toilet and said, "Circle." I'm not sure if he meant the oval bowl or the smaller circle in the center where the water flushes out. Then he put his left hand over his ear, crouched down and flushed the toilet, watching the water circle and then go down the drain. Next he went over to the other stall and did the same thing.

So the afternoon went. He'd run out and play in our room and then all of a sudden head back purposefully into the bathroom. Soon the flushing routine would begin, first in one stall and then the other.

"What do you think we should do about that?" one of the staff asked me as she watched this from the art table where she was working with a group of children.

"I think we'll just let him do it," I said. "It's as if he is running his own desensitization program. He's probably been afraid of the noise of the flushing and now he's worked out his own way to get over it and to conquer his fear."

"It's as if a switch went off in his brain," his mother said at our meeting this week. "All of a sudden he'll go to the bathroom at school and at stores."

How do we explain this? There is an element of magic in it. For weeks nothing seemed to come from all the picture charts and the social story read over and over again. Nothing we could see at least. Then all of a sudden, in some time frame known only to Alex, he got it and the deed was done over and over again.

Sarah Says Hello

Sarah, who has spent so much time repeating the lines she's learned from her musical toys, is now greeting all the teachers in an interesting way.

"Hi Ms. Marion," she'll call out when she comes into the room with Lilly.

"Hi Sarah," I'll call back, "I'm glad to see you."

Then she tries out another name. "Hi Ms. Maria," and then Maria answers from where she is getting snack ready for later in the morning. Sarah goes on naming all of the staff and with our responses she puts together her own Who's Who for the day and locates where we are in the room by the sound of our voices.

Sometimes she'll walk toward the person and reach out her hand to locate them if they are nearby. But more often Sarah stays where she is and calls out to us at intervals to update her sense of where we are in the room.

Writing this I realize that Sarah only greets the adults by calling out their names and that all of her requests are for things she is used to playing alone. Our next steps are clear, to encourage her to call out and locate other children and to have her begin to request activities that involve another child.

We are seeing progress in many ways with Sarah. Yesterday, in the middle of morning circle, she stood up and said, "I want to play the piano."

Maria had offered this choice earlier when Sarah was having her first and, as it turned out, her only tantrum of the day. The tantrum began when we told her it was time to come over to the rug for music time. Sarah refused the suggestion with a firm, "No piano," and immediately sat down on the floor between the cubbies and the rug where we were gathering and began to cry.

She continued to cry in protest as we began to sing. But after a short time I noticed that she was quiet as she listened to the other children singing. When Peter picked the Cookie Jar song to sing next, Sarah couldn't resist the bait and came over to join in the repeated chants of the song. As that song ended, she was ready to take up the offer that had been made some minutes before. The exciting thing for all of us was that she now took the initiative without a cue.

"I want to play the piano," Sarah said, standing up.

"Okay, Sarah – come over here to the piano," Lilly said, using her voice to cue Sarah toward the piano. Sarah walked across the rug and sat down in the cube chair that Lilly had set in front of the keyboard. She played to accompany us on the next three songs that Samuel and

Peter chose and even varied the speed and volume to convey the mounting excitement in one song.

This morning starts out very smoothly. When Sarah first comes through the classroom door with Lilly, she puts her white cane in the corner next to her cubby.

"Good morning, Sarah," I say. "I'm happy to see you!"

Right away she answers "Hi, Ms. Marion," recognizing my voice on the first try.

"I'm going to get Samuel and Peter and Alex," I say, going out the door. "I'll be back soon."

"Bye, Ms. Marion," she says, reaching out her hand to locate me as I pass her.

By the time I come back with the three boys, Sarah is playing a song on the keyboard and singing. When we are all gathered at the rug for music time, I ask Sarah, "Do you want to play piano for us?"

Because she wanted to do this yesterday, I assume that she will happily agree to accompany us again today but things are rarely that simple and predictable.

"All done piano," she says as she stands up. I think she is heading over to her chair for music but somewhere in the transition of a few minutes and six feet across the rug, something goes wrong. Next thing I know Sarah is down on the rug crying, "No, no," and kicking out with her feet.

Lilly tries several interventions. "Want to play the piano?" she asks. "Want to pick the song?"

Both of these ideas are met with more refusals and an escalation of the kicking feet. "No, no," she yells, turning to kick her feet in the direction of Lilly's voice.

So we begin music time with the other children, signaling all the staff to go to "ignore mode". Peter chooses the "Cookie Jar" song and we chant over and around Sarah's protesting little body. In spite of herself, she joins us for a few minutes when Peter hands her the pretend cookie signaling it is her turn. But she doesn't enter in with her usual practice of repeating all the lines, taking both parts.

Then suddenly midway through the next song, Sarah stands up and says," What comes next? Check your schedule."

With that cue, Lilly leads her over to her cardboard schedule board that is sitting on the shelf nearby. Sarah reaches out to touch the objects one at a time while repeating the usual transition routine. "Play piano is all done. Now it is time for music."

As soon as she says this, she sits down in the red cube chair nearby and joins in the rest of the song.

Talking to Lilly and Maria after school, it is clear that our failure to present the schedule board at the transition was what started the whole tantrum. We had not given her the cue to say, "Piano is all done. Check your schedule?" That simple omission of a routine triggered such frustration that she could not recover; had no way to tell us what was wrong. All Sarah could do was to revert to her default behavior of repeated refusals, crying, and kicking out in the direction of anyone trying to offer ideas.

Eliza, our gifted speech therapist, talks about the need to know how to repair communication when an attempt goes awry. Sarah has no ability to repair in the heat of her frustration. It was only later after she had cried and kicked and everyone finally stopped offering wrong solutions that she could come up with her own strategy to repair the misunderstanding. It was as if she reran the video and then spoke both our line and hers to get us back on track.

"What comes next? Go check your schedule board," she said, reminding us what **we** were supposed to say. Only then could she get up and respond with the routine that freed her to sit in her chair and join the music circle.

The Pied Piper

Every day it's been a struggle to get Alex to leave the playground. I was tired of the physical energy it takes and defeated by my inability to come up with a way to help him make the transition. I realized we were floundering and I felt responsible for offering staff more guidance.

At first it seemed tempting to just say that Alex has a problem with transitions. But then I made a list of all the transitions he makes with ease:

- *The walk from the bus to the playground*
- *The walk from the class to the playground*
- *The transition from music circle (not his favorite) to work time at his table (a favorite)*

The list helped me to see that transitions to something he likes go smoothly. But being told it's time to leave the playground is a transition that he resists with all of his energy and ingenuity.

We had already tried using the printed cards to cue him that it was time to go in; an attempt to use his reading skills to enlist his co-operation with our agenda. He liked to read the cards and sometimes it did help. But it was not consistent. Sometimes he just wanted to sit and read the card over and over and then race away from us on the playground, looking back over his shoulder with a grin.

I left school last Friday discouraged, feeling that I had run out of ideas. Sometime over the weekend I remembered that his mother had mentioned that Alex loves Winnie the Pooh music and that she has used it to calm him ever since he was a baby.

Monday morning we found a tape of Winnie the Pooh music and put it in a small tape recorder we had in the closet. We added this to the shoulder bag we carry to the playground every day with first aid supplies and Alex's set of printed cue cards.

When it was time to leave the playground to go in for lunch on Monday, I gave Alex the usual printed card as a cue. He read it but then sat down in the wood chips at the bottom of the slide. This time I picked him up saying, "I'll help you," and moved him out of the playground. He sat down on the asphalt near the playground gate and I waited. After a long stretch of sitting, he stood up and took a few steps toward the school. As soon as he began to move in that direction I surprised him by holding up the little tape player with the Winnie the Pooh song playing. I held it out in front of him and he literally followed the music into school and down the hall to our classroom.

Someone who happened to see this told me later that it reminded her of the story of the Pied Piper.

It worked again at the end of the day when Alex left the playground following the tape recorder that Lilly was carrying as she held his hand and walked toward the bus. "Deep in the Hundred Acre Wood" has become the thing that broke the impasse. I remembered how Alex's mother had told us that he rarely gets a chance to play outside at home. She doesn't feel it is safe to take him to the playground by their apartment when she is alone with him. There is no fence and she wisely doubts that she could keep him safe if he decided to run out.

It is no wonder then that he hates to leave the playground. He loves to run and slide and go in and out of the little playhouse. But he also loves the Winnie the Pooh music and the only time he hears it at school is when he is walking along holding one of our hands, walking along where he needs to go.

Today for the first time he came to me before we began the transition from the playground to lunch. "Open the gate," he said and I realized that it was a request, a signal that he was ready to go and have lunch. So I took his hand and off we went, without the printed card and without the music.

We will see what happens tomorrow.

Watching the Rain

Last week Peter was having a hard time, exhibiting a new resistance to the tasks set out in his four work boxes. He especially resisted doing the verb cards or responding to the sheets of verbal directions he was supposed to follow.

It becomes clear that Peter has settled into a routine. He always wants the boxes to be lined up in the same order and is upset if we set them out in a different sequence. He can't begin work until he rearranges them with the box with the blue square first then the other three shapes lined up in their proper position.

But even when the correct order is established, he has been refusing to do the tasks set out for him. "All done" he will say or simply turn his back on the teacher sitting across the small yellow table from him. All he really wants to do these days is to draw or color in one of the little notebooks we made.

"Peter's notebook," he says proudly each time he finishes filling every page with his colorful pictures.

Yesterday I decided confidently that Peter would do best if I took a turn with him. It started out well enough for the first five minutes but it was downhill from there. Peter wanted to take control of the cards for the lotto game and that was fine for a while. But the whole point was to build his language – not mine. Peter claimed the first set of cards and held one up at a time as he asked me, "What this is?" Then I attempted to take charge of the teaching situation again and asked him to tell me about the pictures in the second set. That's when he crossed his arms across his chest and turned his back on me. If he couldn't have it his way, he was opting out.

It went from bad to worse when he tried to string the shapes that were set out with laces in the next box. The idea was for him to build his fine motor dexterity by working on stringing the shapes. He said "necklace" as soon as he saw them and began to string some onto the black cord. But three shapes into it, Peter had an idea in mind that he couldn't pull off and he became more and more frustrated. He took the shapes off and tried to start again several times, finally crying in complete frustration. All the words I used were of no help. Peter couldn't find any words to tell me what it was he wanted to do and all my attempts to help just made him angrier. I had failed completely and came face to face with my own inability to bridge the language barrier that separated us.

Today is a new day and we hurry to meet the children at the vans, ready to try again. It's raining and going to the playground is not a possibility. Because Sarah is at a Physical Therapy session, I don't want to start our music circle without her and risk throwing off the order of her day. So I decide to stay out in the front entryway to the school and watch the rain with Peter and Samuel. Samuel begins to run to the edge of the portico roof and step out into the rain. When I remark to Lilly that he is flirting with danger, he overhears this remark and it captures his attention.

"Flirting with danger," he calls out as he darts out from under the roof and feels the first raindrops land on his head. After he does this repeatedly, I divert his attention from this game by calling both boys over to look at the wide puddle in front of the school.

"Look it's a puddle," I say, naming it for Peter. "Puddle," he repeats squatting down next to me and watching as I find a small pebble on the sidewalk and throw it into the puddle. We go on to do a verb lesson right there; *throw* for the rocks in the water and *float* for the seeds on top of the puddle.

"Look at the circles," I say, pointing to the circles spreading out from each raindrop. "Bubbles," I comment as we see some of the raindrops make small bubbles on the surface.

"Pop," Peter calls out as he watches them float across the puddle and then break to form more small circles.

Samuel is crouching closer and closer to the puddle watching the circles move across the top of the water. Reaching out to pat my leg where I am crouching next to him, he asks me, "Can rain make squares?"

It's a lesson to me; a reminder that there is a place for the language drills that Peter needed at first to sort out labels for objects and verbs for actions. But as he has made progress, the artificial quality of those exercises is wearing on him and he has shown this in his refusals over the last week. But kneeling by the puddles we've settled into a natural way of naming verbs and commenting on what we observe. Peter joins in eagerly, repeating words that I model for him and then adding his own "pop" as the bubbles burst. Language opportunities are everywhere and the most interesting ones are often spontaneous.

Teddy and the Chocolate Bunny

Teddy carried the chocolate bunny all the way back from California in a plastic bag. His mother tells us that on Easter all he ate was the round chocolate tail before he packed the bunny in the bag his Grammy gave him and saved it for nine days. No wonder he bursts through the classroom door announcing loudly, "I want to show them my _____."

I can't understand the next word at first, but then he says it again using the trick he learned in speech therapy to slow down and say every sound as clearly as possible.

"My cha – ko – lat bunny." Teddy says, pulling the eight inch bunny out of his backpack. The bunny is carefully wrapped and shows little sign of having made the airplane trip from California to Massachusetts.

"I want to share it with my friends!" Teddy announces proudly.

And so it is that we work to cut the chocolate bunny from San Diego into thirteen more or less equal pieces under the watchful eye of Teddy who doesn't want to wield the knife but definitely wants to closely supervise the bunny's transformation. He helps put the chocolate pieces into thirteen small paper cups and we line them up on the counter to save them for snack time in the afternoon class.

The sacrifice on his part is duly noted by at least three of his peers who later report to their parents the amazing fact that Teddy had saved his Easter bunny for nine days and then shared it with all of them.

"And that was a really nice thing for Teddy to do," Maddie announces to a substitute teaching assistant who is with us for the day.

I think of Teddy's Individualized Education Program (IEP) and the goals it includes that he will demonstrate improved social skills and increase the frequency and variety of social/language interactions with peers. I wonder how you quantify this act of friendship; carrying a dark chocolate bunny with blue eyes and a yellow bow tie all the way from California so he can share it with twelve friends.

After we finish cutting the bunny up, Teddy goes to find his backpack where he had left it near his cubby. He pulls out a tattered piece of paper and holds it up for me to see. It is covered with penciled lines going here and there all over both sides of the paper. Along each line he has printed a street name; Pinebrook Lane, Forest River Glen, Overland Drive and on and on.

"It's a map," he says. "This side is California and Grammy and Poppa live on Forest River Glen." Then he flips the paper over and says, "This side is Massachusetts." I see familiar street names spreading in random order across the page.

I remember visiting Teddy at home in September just before he began his second year in our preschool program. His parents were bringing me up to date on the developments of the summer, including his strong interest in dead end streets and songs by the Beatles. The dead end streets are back, but in the months since September he has gained fine motor skills and now spends many hours at home drawing free hand maps and labeling each street, sometimes asking his parents for help with the spelling.

Teddy is outgrowing us. He doesn't need the intensive teaching of our morning class anymore. So over the last two months he has been transitioning to the regular integrated preschool classroom next door.

"Will you miss me when I go to Ms. Ellen's class?" he asks me now each morning.

"Oh yes, I will miss you but I will see you this afternoon."

Today he asked, "Will you miss me when I go to kindergarten when I am five?"

"I certainly will and I'll have to find a way to see you. Will you come and visit us when you are in kindergarten?"

Teddy thinks a minute and then says, "Well I will come to visit but I have to go to kindergarten when I'm five."

I suddenly have the feeling that on Teddy's birthday in May we will have to explain why he doesn't go to kindergarten after he eats his birthday cake. Because on Emily's birthday Teddy told her, "Emily, after you eat the cake, then you will turn to be five!"

Is Today a Jonah Day?

"Is today a Jonah day?" Teddy asks at the end of the morning while he is sitting on the top of the large interlocking rectangle climber set at one end of the preschool playground.

"Yes, Jonah's coming soon. Today's your lunch group with Eliza," I answer.

"I'll watch for him. Sometimes he rides his bike to school and I can see him from up here," Teddy says as he stands up on top of the red panel and turns to look across the street.

I go over to help other children on the slides but I can see Teddy standing and watching the sidewalk for the next five minutes. All of a sudden Teddy breaks into a wide grin and calls across to me, "I see him coming. He really is coming."

With that he kneels down, drops through the hole in the top of the rectangle and climbs out onto the grass. By the time Jonah and his mother come across the street, Teddy is over at the fence calling to him.

"Do you want to play the pizza game?'" he asks. At this invitation from Teddy, Jonah breaks away from his mother and comes over to stand on the other side of the fence. I can't hear what the boys are saying to each other but I soon hear laughter and see them waving their hands in the air as if they are throwing pizza dough.

The pizza game is one of the things they have been playing together this week, a game of their own invention. Eliza introduced them to a pizza board game during the lunch hour social group she has been running for several weeks. Jonah arrives early twice a week and he and Teddy join Eliza for lunch and activities to help them build their social skills.

Jonah arrives each time with his lunch box carefully packed with things he likes to eat. All of the boys unpack their lunches onto the small round table in Eliza's office and Eliza sets her lunch out too. The idea is to use this time for conversation, practicing the back and forth exchanges that don't come naturally to either of these boys. Teddy and Eliza both eat while they do this but Jonah still doesn't eat anything at school. It's hard to know what word to put to this – reluctance, resistance, shyness, or discomfort. It may be that Jonah is simply following a rule he has made that there is no eating at school, his own version of Samuel's rule "Mommies are not at school".

Jonah doesn't eat but he is joining in the conversations more and more each week and soon we begin to notice that he and Teddy are choosing to go to the same area of the room at playtime. I think it is more accurate to say that Teddy chooses where to go and Jonah soon follows him there. It is a solution to Jonah's difficulty deciding what he wants to do when it is "choice time."

"But what should I do," he would ask, unable to choose between the activities we'd offered for that day. Now he tries to wait and see what Teddy chooses and then he says the same thing.

Our dramatic play area is set up as a restaurant these days, complete with a wooden pizza with wedges held together by Velcro. Teddy and Jonah take turns being the one who gets to cut the pizza and then deliver it to the other boy with the pieces piled up in some completely silly arrangement. One of their favorites is to throw all the pieces into a little plastic garbage can.

"Here's your garbage pizza," Teddy called out the first time, proceeding to dump all the pieces onto Jonah's lap. Then it was Jonah's turn and he added a few plastic carrots and a slice of watermelon to the contents of the garbage can.

Sometimes their pizza game gets too wild and silly and one of us has to go over and remind them with some standard teacher comment like "Use your inside voices, please." But even as we try to rein the silliness in a bit, we are delighted to see this friendship emerge and to see Jonah cutting loose and not worrying at all about what he should do.

Samuel isn't so sure about their game, probably feeling left out in some way since Teddy used to spend more time with him.

"There is no such thing as garbage pizza," Samuel calls over to them. "There's pepperoni and cheese and my Mommy has chicken pizza, but there is not garbage pizza."

Teddy and Jonah ignore him as they add even more vegetables to the pizza in the garbage can and take it over to where Samuel is sitting drawing in little notebooks with Peter.

It is only Lilly's quick response that interrupts their plan to dump this in Samuel's lap. "The pizza game stays in the restaurant," she says, steering the friends back to the table set with the red and white checked tablecloth.

"And don't come back," Samuel calls after them, always one to want the last word.

Hot Chocolate and French Fries

The good news is that Alex is beginning to do some simple pretend play. The bad news is that he's completely stuck on one routine. It all started accidentally after he began going over to the dramatic play area each day because he was fascinated by the pretend pizza with six wedges that attach by Velcro in the round pan. He would cut them apart with the plastic knife and take them out and line them up on the table. Then he would put them back in the pan and start the process all over again.

Trying to vary that routine, I asked him to give me the yellow cup.

"Yellow cup," he repeated as he found it on the shelf of the little cupboard.

"Here you go," he said and handed me the cup.

"I want some hot chocolate please," I said, pointing to the toy kettle on the stove.

"Hot chocolate," he said and I showed him how to tip the teapot and pretend to fill my cup. "Here you go," he said after he had done this.

That's when I did something that completely captured his attention and has propelled him through endless repetitions. I pretended to take a little sip, widened my eyes and began to fan my mouth in mock distress.

"It's too hot," I declared dramatically. Alex loved it. "Are you okay," he called out at once.

"I'm okay," I said. "Let's blow on it." Then when we had done that I said, "Let's stir it."

Then I took another sip, declared it delicious and gave him the thumbs up sign to indicate that the drink was now just the right temperature. Then he would excitedly pour me more hot chocolate and hand it to me. His attention was completely engaged as he watched my face intently, eager for the first glimmer of my distress.

He tries it with everyone now. Chris, the speech therapy graduate student working with us this semester, observed this routine on the second day. She was amazed to see Alex's concentration and determination and the emerging imagination.

She joined the game and made the suggestion that we try to vary the theme gradually.

"Just change one thing," she suggested. So we are trying to alternate the hot chocolate distress with hot pizza distress – a variation on the theme. This has only met with moderate success so far. Alex always reverts back to following someone around with the yellow cup in one hand and the teapot in the other.

"Here we go," he'll say, handing the cup to one of the teachers and immediately pouring from the little teapot.

"Hot chocolate," he announces with a twinkle in his eyes, waiting to see if we will join his game one more time.

Then one day he surprised me with a new phrase. "Juggle French fries," he says, handing me six plastic French fries from the play kitchen.

"Juggle French fries?" I ask with a genuinely puzzled expression.

"Juggle French fries," he repeats. So I do and soon the French fries are falling to the floor and it turns out that this is exactly what I am supposed to do. He laughs in delight as he begins to pick them all up. Once he has them all gathered in his hands, he holds them out in my direction again.

"Juggle French fries," he says.

I soon learn that this is the latest version of the hot chocolate game, started when Lilly pretended the French fries were too hot to handle and shifted them quickly from one hand to the other. Alex loved it, dubbed this action, "juggling French fries" and a new game was born.

The Diaper Dash

During choice time, Teddy settles himself at the old round table that he calls our drawing place and most of the other afternoon children call the "crafts table." He is sitting alone next to the large wall of windows that looks out to the hallway. His focus is on a piece of green construction paper in front of him as he is busy drawing or writing. I can't tell exactly what he is doing from the place across the room where I am helping Peter and Samuel begin to build a dinosaur cave from cardboard blocks. Once they have settled into momentary co-operation, I feel free to go over and check in with Teddy to see what he's doing with the green paper.

Along the right side he is printing the days of the week, some repeating and some missing, but so far he has four of them spelled out in his large print.

"How do you spell the next part of Thursday?" he asks me, showing me where he has printed TH. I help him sound out the next letters and he adds those to his list. Then we move on to Wednesday, a word with the strange combination of letters including the N that you never hear.

Along the left side of the paper he's printed a list of months but they aren't in the order of the calendar. He begins with May, a month of great import, because his birthday is May 30th. He has May, June, March, July and August.

"I need some help spelling the 'ber' months," he says, and I wonder for the first time about the derivation of that ending to the months September, October, and November.

Down the middle of the page he has written numbers starting with 1 and counting up from there but adding a "th" after each number; 1th, 2th, 3th, and so on all the way through the teens. His numbers wind back up when they reach the bottom of the page each one followed by the "th". It is a rule he's seen and over generalized, like saying "foots" and "tooths" and "deers". Teddy is storing up information and trying it out as he works to master sequences of the week, the months and numbers.

He chose to work at the drawing table after a circle time that was marked by his almost constant laughter and outbursts of lines of songs or games that he and Jonah have made up. As soon as Jonah arrives for the afternoon the two boys are drawn to each other. As we begin the afternoon's songs they try to catch each other's eye and communicate some uncontrollable silliness with a mere hand gesture, a phrase or by pointing at a picture on the wall.

The social lunch group Eliza has prodded along all year has come to this. These isolated little fellows, each one prone to play alone and diagnosed as "missing social cues" and "lacking social initiation" have now become completely focused on their own particular set of social cues. They could care less about our agenda and our threats to have someone leave circle if they can't calm down.

I think back to the days when Jonah struggled to choose an activity during free choice time. "But what *should* I do?" he would ask. Now here he is disrupting our circle time with his silliness, not at all intimidated by my reminders that he should not be silly right now.

Jonah is too giddy to care because he has been waiting a long time for this. It is too much fun to see Teddy's face light up when he comes in for the afternoon. It is also great fun to have Teddy grab him by the arm and pull him around the room as they point at pictures that have been on the wall since September but now seem to hold some private joke that sends them both into shared laughter all the way to the next picture.

Today the opening music circle for the afternoon class immediately became a time for Teddy and Jonah to resume the repetitive silly songs they seem to have invented overnight. I can't quite get a handle on the words of their newest song. It has something to do with a paintbrush and they mimic painting up and down while the tempo and the volume build in spite of the fact that we are supposed to be singing a very different song.

I spread their name cards out on the rug when I set up for circle before they arrive, but the rug is not large enough to keep them as far apart as we need to in order to interrupt their silliness. Each boy watches for any opportunity to catch the eye of the other and then they launch one of the songs with a simple gesture or by repeating one line in a loud voice.

"The Diaper Dash" is one of their favorites. There are a few other lines but the five year old punch line is "diaper dash". It never fails to get both Teddy and Jonah laughing in a way that soon draws in other children sitting near them.

Our newest child in the class is often drawn to their excitement and once she begins to accelerate, there is no stopping her with words or stern looks. Psychologists call it difficulty with self-regulation or sensory modulation and it operates to varying degrees in all three of these children with a definite multiplier effect.

Even as I work to regain control, or at least some semblance of order, I can't help but recognize the social nature of this chaos. Each of these children has goals in their Individualized Education Program (IEP) that involve paying more attention to peers and engaging in peer interactions and play. And here they are – completely tuned into each other's faces, waiting for a gleam in the other's eye or a few words to set them spilling into a shared silliness that leaves the rest of us behind.

I love what happened earlier today when Lilly was trying to impose some order while I led the songs. She asked another child to move so that she could sit on the rug between Jonah and Teddy, trying to use her own body as a visual barrier. Undaunted, the boys leaned forward or backward just enough to see around Lilly and catch each other's attention. That's all it took and they were off again in one of their private jokes.

Finally, after this had gone on through two songs, I heard Lilly say, "I'm going to have to take one of you out if you can't pay attention."

Jonah stopped laughing for a moment and leaned forward.

"Take Teddy," he said, pointing to his friend.

"It's A Five Birthday"

It's Alex's fifth birthday and he knows that something special is going on. "Happy birthday, Alex," I say when he gets off his van in the morning and then I give him a big hug.

"Happy birthday, Marion," he says returning the greeting without understanding that it doesn't work to repeat this greeting the way he has learned to respond to "Good morning."

So I try to clarify. "No it is **your** birthday," I say, putting my right palm flat on his chest for emphasis.

"It's your birthday," he responds, giving me one of his mighty smiles.

But later when Lilly asks him how old he is Alex remembers a line he must have heard at home. "It's a five birthday," he says, holding up all the fingers on his left hand.

This sequence of exchanges is repeated in more or less the same order several times during the morning as Peter, Samuel and Sarah all wish Alex a happy birthday.

When the afternoon children arrive they are excited that it is Alex's birthday and that his mother is coming later with a cake. One of the girls, Jennifer, arrives dressed in a sleeveless pink floral dress even though it is a cool day. Her mother explains that there was no talking her out of this dress because she wanted to dress up for Alex's birthday.

Later Alex and I take turns reading the book he brought today to share with the class. Alex can read the whole book himself but we take turns because Jonah soon complains that he can't hear the words because Alex reads so quickly in a soft voice.

So I try to read alternate pages but it is soon clear that Alex has to read every page. So sometimes he reads the page first and I repeat it in a louder voice. But then when I go ahead and read the next page, Alex has to repeat that one after me. Fortunately *Where the Wild Things Are* holds everyone's attention and they all try rolling their terrible eyes when we come to that line in the book. Alex has obviously read the book over and over at home. He throws his arm out dramatically as he reads Max's line, "Be still" as if to tame a circle of wild things in front of him.

After the story his mother brings over the cake she's made, all frosted in chocolate with a large number five candle on the top. Of course we can't light the candle at school but it adds to the festivities as we all sing happy birthday to Alex. It seems that it is clearer to Alex by now that this is his birthday and when we finish singing he throws both arms up in the air and says, "Hooray for Alex." All of the children follow him, throwing their arms in the air and calling out, "Hooray for Alex."

Another Surprise

Alex has gone from being a darter to becoming a glider. He moves more slowly and deliberately from one area of the room to another and settles in to an activity for a longer period of time. Peter commented on this the other day after Alex spent twenty minutes playing the hot chocolate game over and over again in the pretend restaurant.

"Alex has more turns," Peter said, "He likes hot chocolate all the time." It was as good a way as any of describing the hold that this repetitive game had on Alex that day.

As a glider Alex is much more available for learning and we are all excited about the changes that are happening in his language and his behavior. He remembers most of the verbs when we show him the pictures for List 1 and List 2 and he is beginning to make spontaneous comments that include verbs. The huge breakthrough that he is now using the toilet at school is further evidence of how far he has come since he darted into our room for his first visits months ago.

There are still times when he exhausts us and when his difficulty managing transitions takes its toll on all of the staff. He is a variable dancer for sure, some days seeming to execute the steps with ease and at other times being completely out of step with the rest of the children.

I had a phone call from his mother two days after she came to help him celebrate his fifth birthday at school. Her voice sounded husky over the phone and I soon realized that she had been crying before she called.

"I can't believe this is happening," she said. "You know that Jeff has been having trouble getting enough hours at work and we have been falling behind in our rent. Well, now everything is coming down on us and the landlord is giving us two weeks to come up with everything we owe him. If we can't do it, then we are going to be out and have to go and live in a house my father owns in Connecticut."

I knew that they had been having problems and that the landlord had given them several warnings, but I hadn't realized how serious things were.

"It may be better," Tara said, "because Jeff can work at the Walmart there and they are promising that he can be full time. The only trouble is that I hate to think of Alex having to change schools just when he is beginning to make progress."

The phone call ended with Tara promising to keep in touch with us and with my suggesting some resources in the community that might be able to help them find another apartment. But I knew that rising housing prices in our town made this a difficult thing to do.

A week later Tara called back with the news that they had a new apartment that would be more affordable and that Jeff had a new job. But all these changes meant they would be moving to a new town and we would be losing Alex. A pall fell over our room the next morning when I told Lilly and Maria that the glider was moving away from us and that there didn't seem to be anything else we could do to prevent it. I had promised Tara that I would call the Preschool Coordinator in their new town and begin to work with her to plan a transition that would be as smooth as possible for Alex.

It all happened remarkably quickly. Lilly made a scrapbook of pictures of Alex and the other children that he could take with him. The afternoon children all wanted to make him a goodbye book and each child drew a picture for Alex. Peter worked carefully drawing a cylinder shape in the middle of his paper and then colored a brown circle at the top.

"It's a cup of hot chocolate 'cause that's her best game," Peter said as he added a blue handle to the cup. I wrote those words on the bottom of the page reminding him though that Alex is a boy so we say "his best game."

"Oh sorry," Peter said in his usually cheerful way. Pronouns continue to confuse him even as his sentences lengthen.

The scrapbook of pictures and the children's drawings were all ready for Alex's last day at our school. Of course Alex didn't have a clue what all the special attention was about. We gave him the books at the story circle, just before snack time.

"Oh wonderful," he said reverting to one of his memorized responses. Then in a return to the phrase that had worked so well for him at his birthday celebration he added, "Hooray for Alex!"

"Hooray for Alex" all the children responded, most of them raising their arms in the air just as he had.

At the end of the day we sent him off on the van for the last time, his extra clothes, his scrapbook and the book of drawings all packed into a large shopping bag we set by his seat.

"Good-bye Alex," I said, checking that his seatbelt was securely fastened. "We will miss you."

"Good bye," he said, completely unaware that there was anything different about this leave taking.

Now we are left wondering what to do with our sense of loss. What do you do with all the hope and love you've invested in a child when he leaves so suddenly? His absence hangs over our daily routines. There were so many times, especially earlier in the year, when we felt exhausted by the stamina it took to help Alex move through a day. But now there is a quiet nostalgia that we all feel for the excitement and the challenge that never failed to be part of our days with Alex. His funny little phrases, his delight in understanding simple directions and his unique talents brightened our classroom every day. And without him here, a special kind of energy and liveliness is missing from our days.

The Newest Child

Andrew is our new child and the intrigue of figuring out how to reach him has captured all of the staff. Yesterday was the beginning of his second week with us. Because it was a rainy day, his father met us in front of the school near the main entrance. He told me that Andrew started to cry the minute they turned right toward the front door instead of going left to follow the sidewalk around to the playground.

Andrew loves the playground and our routine every day last week was to go to the playground first every morning. So that was what he wanted to do yesterday; the fact that it was raining and the playground was soaked from a weekend of rain meant nothing to Andrew. He cried all the way down the hall as I sometimes guided him and at other times had to carry him toward the door to our classroom.

When we finally made it into the room, I helped Andrew take his jacket off and showed him how to hang it in his cubby, my hands over his guiding the jacket onto the hook. As soon as this was done, Andrew took hold of my hand, pulling me toward the door we just came through. He tried in vain to turn the handle but the child proof cover frustrated his efforts. He put my hand on the doorknob making it very clear that he wanted to go back outside.

None of our words made any difference. He does not understand "it's raining" or "later" or "tomorrow." He was one very sad little boy because he wasn't allowed to follow the routine he learned. He couldn't get what he wanted even when he stood by the door and signed "more". It did not work – no one took him to the playground.

Today is bright and sunny and Andrew is smiling as we walk to the playground as soon as he arrives at school. We go around the corner to the back play area where the bikes are lined up on the asphalt riding area. Andrew has developed his own set of routines here. He pays no attention to the bikes or wagons or the little car that is one of Peter's favorites. Andrew likes to sit down in the middle of the asphalt near the grate over the storm drain. He picks out a tiny stone from around the edge of the grate, using his thumb and index finger in a perfect pincer grasp. He drops the small pebble through one square in the grid and watches as it falls down into the water with a silent splash. He works to find another stone and then another until he suddenly jumps up and begins to walk the path through the butterfly garden.

Andrew seems to look at the daffodils and tulips in bloom as he walks by them on repetitions of a route he's established along the grass in front of the library window, over the large rocks and then back to where he started at the top of the grassy slope.

Today he initiates the game we have been working on. He stops at the top of the slope and waits for me to look up at him. As soon as our eyes meet, he starts to run down the hill right at me. I wait until he's four feet away from me, throw my arms out wide and call, "Andrew, come here." He is coming at me propelled by his own energy and the incline of the hill. There is no way he can stop or shift direction so he is compelled to follow the direction "come here" and then I catch him in a hug or spin him around.

The game goes on with Andrew returning each time to the top of the little hill and then waiting a minute before looking at me. It's the game we learned with Alex and now we are passing it on to our newest child. When I go to help redirect some boys from another class who have the wagon at a precarious angle half way up the paved drainage ditch, Lilly tries the game with Andrew. When he looks down and sees her, Lilly calls out, "Andrew, come here." He runs part way down the hill and then veers away from her and heads to the place where I am helping the small group of boys bring the wagon to level ground.

Already we can see that he has learned this routine one way only. He will run to me because I started the game with him but he won't transfer the same game to another person. It is an example of his failure to generalize learning across settings. He learned it as a set and parts can't be changed. We have our work cut out for us!

Yet as I write that phrase "our work" I realize that it will not be my work much longer. Seven weeks from now I will be retiring, leaving the classroom for the last time. This new little guy will be someone else's work. I am just one of those helping to get him started. Lilly and

Maria will stay on but a new teacher will be hired and I will be on my way to whatever comes next.

There is no doubt in my mind about my decision. I am excited about the freedom of it, the lightness ahead. But there are moments each day when I realize how much I will miss. This morning when Peter's mother left him with us for the day, she bent down to kiss him good-bye. They had resolved a minor conflict that had developed on the way to school over a dirty penny that Peter refused to give up to her.

"Be good," she said to him, bending to give him one more kiss.

"I always be good at school," Peter said, throwing his arms out in a wide gesture for emphasis. "I always be good."

I thought how much I will miss these unpredictable moments of honest joy.

Andrew is learning to talk—one word at a time—and that creates new dilemmas. This morning he goes to the gate on the playground, stretches his hand up trying to reach the latch and then says, "Open." Hearing this clear word, I am caught in a dilemma. Our main goal for him is to build communication skills so we want to be sure that his first words are rewarded by obtaining what he wants as often as possible. Frequent reinforcement is important so he will mobilize all the energy it will take him to begin to pair words and actions or words and objects. So when he takes me to the playground gate and says "Open", I open the gate and walk through with him even though that had not been my plan.

"Hold my hand," I say and he does, leading me around to the playground in the back, to the asphalt area for the bikes and wagons surrounded by the grassy hill with the slightly unkempt butterfly garden. He still has no interest in the bikes or wagons. Anytime we coax him over to the bikes and lift him on to a tricycle, he will only sit for a millisecond and then be off and running again.

Today he goes up to the top of the hill and I see him pause and look my way. He is starting the "come here" game again. It isn't completely reliable yet that he will come so I am careful to only call out "come here" when I see that he is close enough to me that I can scoop him up and ensure his successful response to the direction.

It is a lesson in errorless learning that Sara, the Physical Therapist, explained so well to all of us at a staff consult session regarding another child. We need to be sure when we give a direction or ask for a response from a child that the child follows through even if at first we need to coach or prompt that response. Every time Andrew hears the direction "come here" he needs to move toward and connect with the speaker. Eventually that will become such a learned behavior that he will do it automatically when he hears those two words. If we call "come here" and let him run off in the other direction, there is no learning.

Of course one of the problems right now is that he is responding to this command only from his mother and from me but is not carrying it over to other staff. So we begin to try to play the game with two staff working in tandem. I stand near Maria at the bottom of the hill. When I see Andrew look down with that gleam in his eye, I call to him and then, when he runs down, Maria and I swing him together. In theory it sounds good, but this surprising change in the routine seems to catch Andrew off guard and he breaks away from us to head over to the storm grate in search of small pebbles to drop down into the water.

Andrew's new word is to say "bye" to his Dad every morning when he arrives at school as he lets go of his hand and takes mine. Every noon he says "bye" to the teacher walking with him as he takes his mother or father's hand to leave. He says "uh oh" whenever he drops something, "zin" to ask for a turn in the indoor swing that is often our salvation, and "go" when he wants more pushes.

Peter and Samuel are now at the other end of our own version of the autism spectrum, perhaps so far along that they don't even belong on the spectrum anymore. Both of them carry on long, if slightly atypical, conversations as they join in play scenarios that become more complex every week.

I planned to work with Peter today during 1:1 work time because I needed to do some testing for his annual progress report. I was delayed for a while trying to help settle Andrew who was upset that he had to come in from the playground. When I was out in the hall trying to calm Andrew down so he wouldn't disrupt all the other children, I could see Peter through the window settling in at his work table, the four work boxes to his left on the shelf. He was waiting for me to come, the only child in our morning class who could possibly be expected to wait for a teacher.

Maria started over to work with Peter, but then she shifted over to help Samuel because she knew that I needed to get the testing done with Peter today. By the time I finally get there, Peter has taken the card that says "Work Time" off the place where he had matched it to the picture on his table. He is bending the square card in one hand as I walk over to him and it is clear that I have tested his patience.

"I'm here, Peter," I say. "I'm really sorry to be so late."

He holds the rumbled picture of work time out to show me. "I all done work," he says, "cause nobody come work with me."

He has learned all of the routines as our poster child for the TEACCH method of structured teaching. He uses his picture schedule every morning to guide him through the events of each day though he knows the routine by heart now. He took the card from his schedule board and put it on his work table and sat down to work. But what if you do all that and no teacher shows up?

Peter waited and waited and then he took matters into his own hands. That was enough, work time must be over. He had done exactly what he was supposed to do but we didn't follow our routine. Luckily he is still open to beginning with the first box though he notices at once that I've slipped a different activity in there.

He is an amazing boy. When he first began coming to school, he had such limited expressive language that he could not communicate simple requests. His understanding of language was also so tangled he could only follow simple directions when we paired gestures with our words.

Yesterday he came to school and began at once to tell us the story of a bear and her three cubs that had been in his grandmother's yard. The syntax of many of his sentences was still slightly off, but he communicated the whole story.

"Him go up tree – sleep three minutes- come down and take him babies home their house." He then delighted his friends in the afternoon class with the story that "the Mommy come eat the garbage."

A few days ago he picked up one of the lists we keep near the art area with the names of the children in the afternoon class. We use the lists to check off who has completed a project or who is waiting for a turn at dramatic play.

"Okay I take this home?" Peter asked as I saw him scrunching it into his backpack.

"Oh sure, you can have that," I assured him.

Yesterday as he waited for his bus at the end of the day he started rifling through his backpack looking for something.

"Oh no, forgot to give my friends presents," he said as he held out a fistful of oddly shaped papers.

I took one from him and saw that on the front of the paper he had drawn a picture of smiling figures and then had carefully cut around them. On the back he had printed a child's name, all in capital letters. He had 11 of them, one for each child except our newest child Diego who was so new that his name was not on the list Peter had taken home.

"Oh no, I gotta do one for Diego," Peter said when Samuel pointed out to him that he had given one of his pictures to everyone except Diego.

Luckily Diego was calm about it and Peter, looking back over his shoulder as he climbed onto his school bus, called to him, "Don't be sad, I make you one yesterday."

"Yesterday is over," Samuel called back. "You gotta make him one today or tomorrow but yesterday is over."

Peter paused long enough to hear this correction. "Oh sorry, I make one tomorrow."

Sarah and the Beads

It is one of the final days of the teaching career that has been so central to my life for the last thirty years. I've been smiling to myself at times today, excited by the small gains that Andrew is making. The smile is also because I can feel myself stepping back. I don't think that I am doing this in an obvious way that others can see, but I'm aware of watching all the events in this busy classroom and knowing that it will go on without me. For the most part, that is not a sad feeling – just a strange one. There's great freedom and energy in that but I know there will also be ways I will miss being right here in the thick of things.

Yesterday I had a discouraging work session with Sarah. Everything I tried bombed and her resistance and frustration mounted. But this morning I am ready to try again with a new challenge for Sarah. Maria clearly thinks the idea is much too hard for Sarah. She doesn't come right out and say it, but it's obvious as she listens to me explain the new task before school.

I take out a game that has wooden rods set in a rack. Children with sight follow the cards with brightly colored patterns to stack different shapes and colors of beads onto the vertical rods. But Sarah will need to use her hands to feel the pattern of beads on one rod and then replicate it on the other rod.

For the first trial, Maria sets it up with a simple pattern alternating round and square beads. She places Sarah's hands on the bottom of the rod to her left and helps her feel along the stack of four beads.

"Round, square, round, square," Maria narrates as she guides Sarah's hands to touch each bead. Then she moves Sarah's hands to the empty rod to the right and says, "Match beads."

Sarah hesitates just a minute and then begins to explore the beads in the tray in front of the rods. When she finds a round bead she turns it in her hands, feeling for the hole in the top. Holding the bead in one hand, she reaches out with the other to locate the empty rod. Then she slides her hand to the top of the empty rod and works and brings the bead in her other hand over to fit the rod into the hole in the bead. When she opens her hand, the bead slides down the rod.

The habitual shaking of her head from left to right has stopped as she concentrates on the task, working until she finishes matching the pattern of four beads. Maria and I exhale, realizing we have both been holding our breath as we watch Sarah meet this new challenge.

"I did a good job," Sarah announces as she finishes.

"You did an excellent job," I say quietly, "You made the pattern."

Later when she's having snack with the other children, Lilly asks, "What did you do at work time today Sarah?"

Sarah is quiet for a few minutes and then surprises us all by announcing, "I did the pattern game."

Meeting Season

It is nearing the end of the school year and every Friday a Team Meeting is scheduled to review the progress of one of the children and to plan ahead for what they will need next year. It's a time for the teacher and all of the specialists who work with a child to meet with the parents and discuss the next steps. There is a tremendous amount of work this time of year because there is always testing to be done, a report to be written and then a new Individualized Education Program to be drafted after each meeting.

But there is no doubt in my mind that this is one of the strong protections of the Special Education legislation, state and federal, that guarantees a "free and appropriate education" for children with special needs. The mandate to meet annually to review a child's progress and write a new educational plan for each year protects children from the warehousing and neglect that was often the experience of children with disabilities before the passage of federal legislation.

Teddy's meeting is one of the first and I begin to get ready to write his annual report by going back and reading the reports we all wrote a year ago. Then I go through the data on his progress, the anecdotal records and the progress report that I wrote at the mid-point in his year. He has made so much progress that it's exciting to be able to record and document those gains in his report. Sometimes the process is not so affirming and I am forced to look at what else we may need to do to help a child make more gains. But in Teddy's case we come to the meeting date with a sense of awe at all that he has accomplished in the past year and with confidence that he is ready to move on to the new challenges of kindergarten next year.

Sitting in the same conference room where we first met with Teddy's parents over two years ago now, I remember how I wondered then if I had the energy and the insight to help design and implement the intensive program that Teddy would need. I was beginning to look toward retirement and had times when I doubted my staying power to see this program through. Now here we are reviewing all the progress Teddy has made and sharing the rich history of these two years of working together. I wouldn't have missed it for anything retirement may have to offer. Teddy's parents have done an amazing job of providing a host of rich experiences that have helped him grow and develop.

Peter's meeting also goes well and everyone agrees that he is ready to be in the regular kindergarten class next year with continuing support from the Speech Therapist. Our assumption is that he will be able to join in the activities of his kindergarten class and continue to build his readiness skills right along with the group. If it turns out that he needs more help, the team can meet again next year and build in more services. But we expect that he will be able to be successful in the kindergarten and has moved beyond the need for intensive special education services. A success story for sure!

Samuel will also go on to kindergarten next year and we are not recommending support services from the teacher who works with the older children with autism spectrum disorder. This is not to say that he won't present challenges to his next teacher but they will be more in the area of behavior management and fostering social skills. The teacher who will receive him next year is a master at helping children with those kinds of issues so we know that Samuel will be in good hands.

The hardest report for me to write is Sarah's because I am not sure what I think the best recommendations are for her for next year. In so many ways, it seems to me that she is just settling into the routines of our class in the morning and Louise's integrated preschool in the afternoon. Louise reports the progress she is making in joining the afternoon circle and interacting more with other children. I see the advances she is making in the morning class and wish that she could have another year to consolidate these gains before going on to the increasing demands of kindergarten.

But I know that her parents are completely committed to having her go to kindergarten next year at her neighborhood school where her brother is a second grader. It is the school where I taught preschool for fourteen years before coming to start the autism program here and I know that it is also a wonderful, welcoming school.

On the day of Sarah's meeting, Eliza, Louise and I drive together to the meeting that has been set at their neighborhood school. It is so familiar to me to drive the route to the school where I taught for so many years and I remember the excitement I felt so many mornings anticipating another day with children and colleagues I loved.

We are directed to a classroom upstairs where a long table is soon lined on both sides with teachers, therapists, a psychologist, the Special Education Director and Sarah's parents. As the meeting goes on it becomes clear to me that it has already been decided that Sarah will go on to kindergarten at this school honoring her parent's strong preference. It isn't my decision to make, so all I can do at this point is to present my ideas about what teaching strategies work best with Sarah. Louise offers to be available in any way that will be helpful to the team that will be working with Sarah next year. As I listen to the staff talk about their plans for helping Sarah learn her way around the new school in September, I realize that it's time for me to let go. Now it is someone else's turn to answer Sarah's question, "What do you want to do?"

The Boxes

The day's work is done, all the chairs are put up until tomorrow and I'm going home earlier than usual. My colleague Ellen from the class next door is coming over for tea and the transfer of theme boxes collected over twenty years. They line one wall of our garage; the dinosaurs in the clear box that stacks on the blue tub labeled Police/Fire. Science sits on top of the construction sets, and dress-ups vie with extra clothes for space above the grocery store box and the doctor's office.

Twenty years of small budget orders can still add up to fill the side wall of a garage. I realize I am nostalgic as I carry them out one at a time, sometimes stopping to check what is really inside a particular box. Ellen's five-year-old son, Ryan, is at my elbow, eager to open the small box on the top of the science bin. He carefully takes off the rubber bands that hold it secure. I can't remember how long ago I put this safely away. We are both surprised when he opens the lid of the small box and there are ten small polished stones. On top there is a list written in my younger hand with the name of each stone beside a few words of description.

Ellen lines each box up until her truck bed is full. We are left with a few boxes for a later date. The extra winter clothes she doesn't want will go to the Salvation Army. The costumes will stay until we've used them with the cardboard castle the children will finish painting tomorrow.

The truck is loaded with the accumulated wealth of parent donations. Menus, chef's hats and order pads from the father who managed a restaurant. Scrubs, x-rays and ace bandages from the parents who are doctors, nurses and lab techs. The garage is suddenly larger and the storage capacity renewed. There is a surprising lightness to this passing on of the boxes.

Earlier Ellen stood next to me in my study as I pulled books from the shelves, *Art for Children, Bubbles, Magnets and Goop, The Activity Centered Curriculum*. One by one I handed them over to her, some so obviously unmarked I should have been embarrassed but all I did was laugh.

I'll keep the books that line another shelf upstairs, the autism books, the last frontier of my teaching career. That interest took over so that the newest art and science books were rarely used. I relied on my past experience to generate the ideas for the general activities of the lively afternoon class.

My time over the last seven years was claimed by the endless demands and challenges of figuring out how to reach Sarah and Alex or Luis, Teddy and James. Yesterday I seriously wondered if I had the energy and patience to make it through twenty four more days until retirement. Today that seems like a ridiculous statement. I've taught for thirty years in one setting or another and of course I can make it through twenty four more days.

The Last Day Comes

We are getting ready for the end of the school year party this afternoon. It will be my last, the end of my long string of years teaching, each year ending with a family celebration. Songs will be sung and we will present each child with a scrapbook of their own artwork and photos taken over the course of the year.

But first thing this morning, before we settle into the last flurry of getting ready, we head for the playground with the children of the morning class. Samuel has run ahead with Lilly close behind him. Sarah has gone inside with Maria to have some time to play the keyboard and be ready for music time when we come in.

Peter walks beside me talking all the way, sometimes holding Andrew's hand for as long as he will let him. All Andrew has said so far this morning is "bye bye" to his mother when she left him. Peter talks constantly as we walk and I remember when he first came and had so few words that he couldn't let us know what he wanted and would have to revert to tantrums almost daily in his frustration to be understood.

Now he is talking away, telling me that he left his new backpack at his Grandma's house yesterday so that is why he's carrying a new lunch bag in one hand. The day is already warm so when we are near the gate into the playground I say, "Peter, put your lunch bag in the shade."

"What you mean shade?" Peter asks.

I show him the part of the grass that is darker, in shadow, not sunny; using different words to try to explain the concept of shade. He seems to understand because he puts his lunchbox next to Andrew's backpack in the shady area near the gate. Samuel calls to him from the top of the climber and he is off to join him.

Later, after he and Samuel have been up and down the slide and running around the playground, Peter comes over to complain of the heat this morning.

"Let's go over in the shade by the tree," I say, walking toward the pine tree near the sandbox. Peter follows me and looking up at the tree ahead of us says, "Tall tree."

As soon as we are in the shaded area under one side of the tree, Peter feels the difference in temperature and smiles.

"This is night-night," Peter says when he is in the cool dark space. "Night-night," he says again. He has the mind of a poet, I think, recently given words to tell us his thoughts.

Andrew is still in a very different place as he comes to take my hand and pull me toward the gate to get out of the playground. "Open" he says and we are through the gate and headed back to the class for music time.

After lunch Teddy is watching for Jonah to arrive for this last day of school. We usually have our music circle and meeting time first. But today the music time will be later after families and friends arrive to join in the celebration. We go outside to the playground first and Teddy stands on top of the climber hoping to catch a glimpse of Jonah and his mother walking to school. Meanwhile he is playing with Samuel and they are taking turns speeding down the tunnel slide.

Samuel spots Jonah first when he is still riding his bike down the sidewalk toward school with his mother behind him on her bike.

"Here he comes," Samuel calls out to Teddy and both boys run over to stand by the fence, calling to Jonah as he crosses the street and comes toward the playground. Soon all three of them are back up on the climber. I have no agenda to impose so I am free to climb up onto the platform when Teddy calls down to me, "Get on – we're going on a plane."

I climb up to where Teddy maintains control of the steering wheel next to the tunnel slide. "Sit there," Jonah tells me, pointing to the top step that functions as a bench.

"All aboard," Teddy calls out, pumping one hand above his head as he mixes train language into the airplane game.

"Put on your seatbelt," Jonah says to me with a serious look on his face so I move my hands and make a click as if to do just that. Jonah smiles his wide and approving smile and then turns his attention to Samuel who is sprawled out on the platform near our feet.

"Samuel," Jonah announces, "I am the seat belt guy and you got to wear your seat belt."

Samuel raises his head up to look straight at Jonah who is trying to look as officious as he can. Samuel opens his mouth, bares his teeth for a moment and growls, "Dragons don't wear seat belts."

This is said with such an air of authority that the seat belt guy relents. "Well just stay on that floor then and don't scare anybody else. We are almost there."

Teddy steers the plane to a safe landing and announces that we have arrived. The dragon goes down the slide first and Teddy and Jonah soon follow.

It is time to go inside and celebrate the last day with family and friends. For so many years I have been a teacher who carries children home with me each night, on my mind or in my heart or in some deep and discouraged place when I am troubled about what to do next. Eventually I've always found the spark in them that ignites some new energy in me. Sometimes that has been enough to unlock something and set a child in motion on a journey to results, to being able to do things they could not do before. I have always come back for another year, to another group of children who I barely know in September but will know so well by June. The bait always tempted me out of the shade of summer back into the new beginnings of fall.

But today I will step down, say good-bye to dragons and seat belt guys, to hot chocolate and juggling French fries and to singing songs while Sarah plays the keyboard.

"Come on," Samuel calls to me impatiently from the bottom of the slide. "We already landed. We're all done."

I bend my tall frame and head down the tunnel slide for one last ride before I join the children lining up to go inside for the celebration.

Later at the end of the afternoon, Luis suddenly appears at our door. On the way back to his class across the hall he looked through the window and noticed children and families eating cookies and drinking lemonade.

"Who has a birthday?" he calls out as he comes through the door.

"It's not anyone's birthday, Luis," I say, walking over to greet one of our favorite graduates. "It's the last day of school for the preschool today."

"Oh, I'm going to miss you," he says, not quite sure how else to respond.

"Well I am going to miss you too," I say, not sure how else to express all that I feel.

Appendix: Information about the Classroom Model

Our understanding of autism and the accepted diagnostic labels evolved over the course of my career as a teacher of young children. When I taught in an integrated preschool in the early 1980's, we had two children who were labeled "autistic." We understood autism to be a developmental disability caused by abnormalities in brain structures or function. But our expectations for those children were limited by the label they carried.

By the mid-1990's, young children with a constellation of problems including speech/language delays, limited social interactions and repetitive and unusual behaviors were often given the label of Pervasive Developmental Disorder (PDD). Children with higher language skills but difficulty with social interactions and restricted patterns of language and behavior were given the diagnosis of Asperger Syndrome. The classic autism label was more often reserved for children with the most severe limitations.

With the May 2013 publication of the DSM-5 diagnostic manual, the diagnostic categories were revisited and changed. All autism disorders now fall under the umbrella diagnosis of autism spectrum disorder (ASD). This includes children with a range of needs from classic autism to what was formerly called Asperger Syndrome or high functioning autism.

Preschool children with significant language and social delays are often referred by their pediatricians for an evaluation by a developmental clinic or a neurologist. Children who leave these evaluations with the diagnosis of autism spectrum disorder (ASD) also come away with recommendations for specialized educational services.

There is general agreement that intensive early intervention leads to the greatest progress for children on the autism spectrum but there are divergent approaches to teaching children with autism. Many parents are first introduced to one of the predominant philosophies if their child is in an Early Intervention (E.I.) program for children from birth to three years old. Some parents read and research on their own and become strong advocates for one approach. In some cases parents and Early Intervention staff are committed to an Applied Behavior Analysis program with systematic teaching using discrete teaching trials. Other families are strong advocates for the Floortime therapy of the Developmental Individual-difference Relationship-based model (DIR) created by child psychiatrists Stanley Greenspan, M.D. and Serena Wieder, PhD. In North Carolina preschool programs are designed according to the TEACCH model developed at the University of North Carolina and implemented throughout that state.

Like most school systems around us, we had a "one size fits all" approach to serving young children with special needs. We provided a half-day preschool program four times a week for a total of ten hours of service. Within these ten hours children also received the related services they needed including Speech/Language, Occupational and Physical Therapies. All of our preschool classes were integrated because of our firm belief that all children benefit from learning from and with peers and the legal mandate to provide services in "the least restrictive environment."

By the mid-1990's the growing research in the field contributed to our awareness that the standard preschool program we were providing was no longer "best practice" for children with an autism spectrum disorder. I requested a sabbatical to study educational models for serving young children with ASD. I was given the public school version of a sabbatical – a year's leave without pay!

This freedom from being in the classroom allowed me to spend a year visiting other programs, attending conferences, workshops and trainings. I researched several of the most respected approaches and, as the year progressed, we began to develop a model for an expanded preschool program to serve the children in our city who had an autism spectrum disorder.

In designing the new intensive program we were strongly influenced by the TEACCH model developed at the University of North Carolina. The TEACCH model is based on the philosophy that there is a "culture of autism" and that often people with autism share common characteristics in their learning style. TEACCH asserts that educational programs should be designed to capitalize on the strengths of this learning style including strong visual skills and memory, a preference for routines and a drive to complete tasks that are presented clearly.

The program we designed was based on many aspects of the TEACCH model including the use of visual schedules and cue cards, intensive one to one teaching using a structured teaching system with visual cues, and the teaching of independent work skills.

We came to feel strongly that the program we were designing also needed to incorporate aspects of two other approaches to teaching children with autism, Applied Behavior Analysis and the Floortime model. The individual and complex needs of each child required that we combine ideas and strategies from several teaching approaches because each one offered something different that strengthened our model.

The program provided a full day at school for children from three to five years old who met the criteria for intensive intervention. The program was rich in staff to support intensive teaching in the morning class. I was the lead teacher and had a staff that included two talented assistant teachers, Lilly Pastor and Maria de la Vega. Other teaching assistants worked with us in the years before the stories in this book and each person brought skills and insights that enriched the program. Eliza D'Agostino, an experienced Speech/Language Pathologist, was instrumental in helping us develop this program.

In the mornings the children attended a small Special Education class that included from three to six children at a time. The schedule of the morning was highly structured and consistent from day to day. Each child had a visual schedule with pictures or objects arranged from left to right to show the sequence of their day. Children joined in a music circle where picture cards or objects representing each song were used to allow non-verbal children to choose a song. Singing was always accompanied by actions and/or sign language so various levels of participation were available.

During one to one work time each morning a series of tasks were presented using the work system and visual cuing of the TEACCH model. The work included direct teaching sessions using techniques drawn from the discrete trial format of Applied Behavior Analysis programs. But there were also language activities that were more naturalistic.

Each child had a detailed work plan for the week that guided the systematic teaching of skills that addressed the goals in their Individualized Education Program (IEP). We developed systems for recording data on each child's progress with assistance from two autism consultants, Kathleen Salomone and Gillian Fahmy, who worked with us. The work plans, data sheets and anecdotal notes were maintained in a notebook for each child so we had a systematic record of their progress to guide the next steps.

Because many children on the autism spectrum don't develop social awareness and play skills in the natural progression that other children experience, we also included guided play sessions each morning to begin to build social and play skills. As we worked to build social engagement and early reciprocal play, we were using techniques from the "Floortime" model developed by Drs. Stanley Greenspan and Serena Wieder.

Everything in the morning program, including outdoor play time, snack and lunch was seen as an opportunity to build the communication and social skills that the children needed to progress. We were also teaching the attending and learning behaviors that allowed the children to begin to expand their cognitive skills.

The energy level rose dramatically in the afternoon as we welcomed the "afternoon kids," a group of four- year old peers who were either typical learners or had milder special needs. Everything we did in the morning was designed to support the children with ASD participating in the afternoon program as best they could and to support their learning from the experiences they shared with typical peers.

The afternoon began with a music circle with the larger class of children that repeated the routines and song choices that had been used in the morning with the children with ASD. In a very real sense, the morning was a pre-teaching session that prepared them for the afternoon. Small group activities followed circle time and were designed to engage the children with special needs in language, arts and creative play activities with peers who served as role models. The afternoon session also included extended choice time when children explored the rich environment of the well-equipped preschool classroom. Teaching staff were often engaged in facilitating play for the children with ASD, at times using other children as coaches to help the children with ASD participate.

Each child's program was based on their IEP and therapies were provided in accordance with that plan. All of the children received Speech and Language Therapy both in the classroom and in a separate therapy room. Some of the children also received Occupational Therapy and Physical Therapy to address sensory and motor deficits and to help them gain processing and motor skills.

The teaching team benefited from the consultation and modeling provided by very talented therapists who worked with us. Often therapists worked with children in the classroom so we were able to observe the techniques they used. This supported carryover of therapies into the classroom activities of each day. At other times, children went to a therapy room where special motor equipment was available or where a quieter environment aided speech and language work.

Each child had a communication notebook that traveled to and from school most days. Teachers and therapists used this to share notes about the school day and ask or respond to questions. Often parents shared information about activities at home that helped us build conversation or respond to phrases that a child was using.

Early in my career as a special education teacher I had learned how important a partnership with parents is to support the progress of the children in my class. One year I had two children referred to our class from the Early Intervention program who presented new challenges for me as a teacher. Each of them had a different rare disease that caused very significant delays in their development and would result in a progressive loss of functioning. I remember going to observe one of the children at her playgroup with the EI program soon after she was referred. I came away feeling inadequate to meet the needs of this little girl because I knew so little about her genetic disease.

What I soon realized was that for almost three years her parents had been learning all they could about her disease and had become experts in accommodating her needs. They became my teachers, sharing the information they had gathered. My role was to take that information and put it to use as I welcomed their daughter into a preschool program that would be the only opportunity in her short life to attend school with her peers. She thrived as she joined in group activities, using her signs to communicate with the other children who eagerly learned basic sign language. Later when she could no longer stand to walk, another child would sometimes crawl with her as she made her way across the room on her knees.

The communication books were a tangible sign of the importance of communication between home and school. Parents of children with special needs including autism spectrum disorder are often experts at understanding and interpreting their child's behavior and needs. Partnership with parents was critical to the success of the program that was the setting for the stories in this book. Each child's progress depended on that partnership and I am deeply grateful to the parents for sharing their insights and understanding with me. Most of all, I am grateful to them for sharing their children!

Where to begin to find more information:

For further information about autism spectrum disorder and the educational approaches mentioned in this book, your public library is an excellent place to start.

Your pediatrician or your local public health facility can refer you to the Early Intervention program that serves your community. Early Intervention is a system of services that helps babies or toddlers with developmental delays.

Special education services for preschool children from three to five years of age with disabilities or those who are experiencing developmental delays are provided free of charge through your public school system. These are mandated by the federal law entitled the Individuals with Disabilities Education Act or IDEA.

Internet Resources include the following:

1. Information, education, support and advocacy for children and families with Asperger Syndrome or autism spectrum profiles is available at Asperger/Autism Network https://www.aane.org
2. General Information about autism, descriptions of educational models and resources for parents: Autism Speaks https://www.autismspeaks.org
3. Information about the TEACCH Program and their model for structured teaching https://www.teacch.com/
4. Information about "Floortime" and the Developmental Individual-difference Relationship-based model (DIR) created by child psychiatrists Stanley Greenspan, M.D. and Serena Wieder, PhD. http://www.icdl.com

Author's Appreciation

First of all, I am deeply grateful to all the children and families who taught me so much over the years and enriched my life enormously. Only a few of you appear in these stories, but all of you have a place in my heart.

I owe many thanks to two groups of people, those who were part of living these stories, and those who sustained me through the writing. I have been supported and encouraged every step of the way by Michael Kane, my partner through both the living and the writing of these stories, and so much more.

My sons Will and Chris introduced me to the fascinating world of how young children learn and started me on the path to my career. Our three grandchildren Eric, Eli and Sophie and my daughter-in-law Anne expanded my understanding of and delight in how children grow and become strong and unique individuals. I am sustained in so many ways by my large and loving extended family who encouraged me by asking just often enough, "How is your writing going?" Special thanks to my sister Sarah Margaret Bartlett for her careful editing of the final draft.

During the years of writing this book, I was guided and encouraged by writers who shared their skills, insights and friendship. It began as fragments written during Tuesday night workshops with Patricia Lee Lewis at Patchwork Farm. Arriving after a busy day of teaching, I would often find that the children had followed me there and waited to appear in their stories. My deep gratitude to Patricia and the members of the group who asked to hear more.

Great Darkness writing group sustained and encouraged me through the years of completing these stories. My thanks to all of you for believing in this book even when I doubted it: Marianne Banks, Joan Barberich, Jennifer Jacobson, Celia Jeffries, Lisa Drnec Kerr, Patricia Lee Lewis, Alan Lipp, Edie Lipp, Patricia Riggs, Jacqueline Sheehan, and Morgan Sheehan-Bubla.

We all cherish our years of writing with Jeanne Borfitz and her loving legacy goes on.

Dori Ostermiller and her manuscript group at *Writers in Progress* helped me begin to shape a pile of stories into a coherent manuscript.

The women of Voices from Inside often inspired me with the honesty and beauty of their writing. My thanks go to them for teaching me about the power of story to change lives.

Early childhood teaching is a team effort and I am indebted to all the colleagues who helped shaped this program. During the period of these stories, Lilly Pastor and Maria de la Vega were key members of the teaching team, contributing their skills, insights, and patience. In the earlier years of this program, there were other very talented teaching assistants who helped to refine the model and I am indebted to each of you for the part you played in helping create this program.

Eliza D'Agostino, a gifted Speech/Language Therapist, contributed her experience, sensitivity and boundless energy. The foundation of my understanding of language acquisition was laid during my years working with Betty Musante, a masterful Speech/Language Therapist and advocate for children.

The skills and expertise of Occupational Therapist Stacy Noble and Physical Therapist Sara Harvey are reflected in the description of these years.

Kathleen Salomone and Gillian Fahmy both served as consultants to the program and were immensely helpful in guiding us and refining our understanding of children with ASD.

Barbara Black has been a colleague and friend for many years and her sensitivity to the needs of children and families is a model for all of us who have worked with her. My thanks to Gwen Agna, principal extraordinaire, for her leadership and guidance.

My Women's Group, past and present, listened to me wrestle with finding time for teaching, writing, family and activism and helped me find a way to balance them all. My thanks to Lourdes Mattei, Lynn Matteson, Dale Melcher, Lydia Nettler, Sue Schwartz, Patricia Wachter, Joan Wiener, and Vicki Van Zee.

Dorothy and Jenny never lost faith in this project and were the "midwives" who encouraged me to finally give it birth.

My thanks to Glenn Ruga for a cover design that introduces the stories inside. Finally, my deep appreciation to Steve Strimer and all the staff of Levellers Press for your commitment to publishing and the skills that made this book a reality.